The Revisionist Volume 1:

A Tale of Three Mothers

W0006195

By: *Michael A. Delitala*

Dedicated to Carmen Delitala

For the two Dr. Cohens in my life.

Table of Contents

Chapter 1

"You know Gavino! We're not assholes...or something!"

That's my dad; explaining to his adult son over the phone, that at his inflexible age of 64, and at my prime age of 37, that he and my unworldly stepmother are not "assholes". About the 17th time, and at about the third iteration of that phrase throughout my life, I started to really question my upbringing, present day circumstances, and conversations, and whether or not I had enough evidence to make the opposing argument to tell my parents that they are indeed - *assholes*.

This reflection, this introspection has not been without a price. Memories and events that I had purposefully buried deep within my unconscious, have resurfaced and I feel inclined to address my past within the present.

For example, I find that I am having fake dialogue with the parents at random moments and in random places. Yesterday, while rinsing off the suds on my body within the shower, my dad and I began an argument about the lack of last names on wedding invitations for a wedding that took place greater than three years ago. Shortly after, while driving into work, I had a shouting match with my stepmother regarding the apology she still owes my wife for the way my wife was treated by *her* side of the family at a Thanksgiving dinner.

These are *real* arguments and *real* dialogue causing physiological changes to my disposition. The blood pressure spikes. There are emotional outbursts. There is thought in anticipating the next random, ridiculous, assholish statement that will come out of a conservative and retired mind and in turn, there is a response waiting on the tip of the tongue. But they aren't really real and there has yet to be direct interaction or confrontation. There will be.

But of course it goes deeper than what I've superficially presented thus far. My wife and I have been married for greater than three years. She's 33 and her name is Doyoung. She is Korean by name and ethnicity but was raised from infancy in America by adoptive, older, Caucasian parents. We have a great life together in southern California and are the proud parents of a French Bulldog named T'Pol. Yes, she's named after a Vulcan officer from the Star Trek – Enterprise series (which, in my humble opinion, is the best Star Trek series to date). Anyway, Doyoung is in the process of getting her second law career off the ground and I am continuing an inspiring career in the pharmaceutical industry. We are reaching a point in our marriage and in our life where we inevitably center our discussions on children: To have or not to have, that is our question.

We believe we want one child. Not so secretly, I joke with Doyoung that I am looking forward to the twins she will bear us. I can settle with one but I'm hopeful for two. Deciding on when to have the child and deciding that we want a child are easy decisions relative to a third: How will we parent these children (or the child). What will be our practices and our parenting philosophy?

We both agree that we want to be better parents than our parents were to us. We say things like, we'll have more money than they did and therefore we will be able to provide better opportunities for little Giovanni or little Stella. We're going to send them to camps. They're going to be a rock star. Or a famous actor. Or a scientist. Or a lawyer. Something prestigious and lucrative where they can make it in this world and not struggle as much as we did and have. We're certainly not going to be assholes to our kid! But one thing is clear, they are NOT going to spend any time alone with my parents, their grandparents because...

"You know...we're not assholes or something."

My dad is of Italian heritage. He was born in Liberia, Africa to a military brain surgeon and a government language translator. My dad's dad, who I should know as my grandpa, was a military

3

brain surgeon with high blood pressure and subsequently stroked out and died before my dad turned two years old. My grandma, who the whole family believes was a spy in her heyday, speaks six or seven different languages, and in her late twenties or early thirties found herself to be a widowed, single mother of one.

A few years after my father's father passed away, my grandma remarried a younger man. She married a tall, dark, and handsome Air Force Sergeant who I know as my grandpa. Shortly after they were married, he received orders to relocate to the United States. They relocated to what is now a shut down air force base in the Upper Peninsula of Michigan. And for the majority of my father's childhood, the substantial years anyway, he was raised there along with three half-brothers and one half-sister.

My dad was raised in a time where money was sparse for an enlisted man such as my grandpa. In fact, it was a point of contention for my grandfather, who on more than one occasion, complained to the family that "if only he had gotten more education" then he could have been something more in the military. Clearly, that was the military's fault. Anyway, my grandma would work odd jobs on the base to pull in some extra cash and for all intents and purposes, together they made the ends meet. When they were married, my grandma took my grandpa's German last name for her own, but she left my father's Italian heritage intact by allowing him to keep his biological father's name. Apparently grandpa was cool with it too. Thus, I get to be of Italian heritage, mostly in name, thanks to her progressive thinking.

It's a running joke in our family, the story of grandma and grandpa and the circumstances by which they met. Grandma is 100% Italian and has a gargantuan temper for being all of five-feet nothing, and a mere 100 lbs. Grandpa, on the other hand, is 100% German, approximately 6'4", and in his prime, was a solid, muscularly 210 lbs. Family reunions are hilarious in appearance. You have the one side of the family being half-German / half-Italian giants and by comparison, the other side have the appearance of full blooded hobbits – including the copious amount of foot hair.

My dad was raised with a Catholic background however, as the story goes, the family didn't practice much. In her deep Italian accent, my grandma would say, "Gavi! You look under that rock over there. You'll find Jesus. Serious". She was trying to tell me that you don't need to go to a church to have faith in God. My dad went to school at the local, public school and was a straight-A student excelling in the sciences. He was handsome, smart, and popular. In high school he played football and wrestled. He would be proud to tell you three things:

I was the oldest; I always took care of my younger brothers and sister. I helped bag groceries at the local PX and ran a paper route right up until I left for college and helped contribute financially to the house. When I played football, boy, let me tell you, I was the fastest kid on the team. (the smallest too; no one could find me).

Anyway, near the end of high school my dad joined the local ROTC program and had aspirations of becoming a military officer. Due to some glitch with my dad's citizenship paperwork, the military "refused his application", and for my dad, that was the end of a prospective military career. Instead of joining the military, he moved to south Michigan and attended a Detroit university obtaining a Bachelor of Science in Chemistry. He was the first member of the entire family, any side, to receive a college education. Upon graduating, he stayed local and found himself able to work in the paint business for what is still a reputable corporation. In fact, and at this point, if you have an older vehicle, the paint you have on the exterior was mostly likely designed and manufactured under the auspices of my father.

At some point shortly after graduating from the university, my dad fell in love with what I know to be my biological mother, got married, and a little less than nine months later I was born. My mother was not an attractive woman by most men's standards and I have never been able to determine what about her drew my father's attention. Since I have to guess, it was probably only intended to be a sexual relationship. A way for my dad to get his "little carrot" wet. She had long, jet-black hair, with brown eyes, pale complexion and a nicely shaped face. Her face was her best feature so perhaps my dad, in his younger years, was a "face-guy".

She was not physically active and as a consequence became rotund. She was five-feet nothing and about 250 lbs. During their relationship, my dad was a little guy being five-foot-four and roughly 125 lbs. When it was still funny to him, he liked to joke, "Jack sprat could eat no fat, his wife could eat no lean. So betwixt the both you see, they licked the platter clean". Immediately followed by, "Hey hey hey", which of course is a Fat Albert reference.

To my knowledge, my biological mother grew up in inner city Detroit and barely graduated high school. And other than what I remember of her stepfather and her mother, I really don't know much else about her upbringing or her life before me. Her parents rarely had any interactions with me so for the most part, there ends their part of this story.

There is little known to me about what happened in my infant to toddler years but I have been told stories from my Aunt and Uncles from my father's side.

Shortly after the birthing event, as I am told, my biological mother developed mental instability and must have perceived me to be some kind of foreign entity. Speaking without first-hand knowledge, it is apparently a miracle that I am alive today and physically unscarred. The biological mother attempted to kill me through stabbing, drowning, electrocuting, burning, and suffocating. In each attempt, it is by sheer luck, or coincidence, or synchronicity that someone or something was able to intervene. For example, in the drowning attempt, my Uncle happened to walk in as I was being held under the water and as he describes, "I was sure the last of your breaths were drawn but low and behold, when I wrestled you away from your mother, you started breathing again". Even as an infant I was rebellious with a passion for living.

I do not care to describe each event and the second hand story herein. I do care to say that this kind of intervention or luck has followed me throughout my 37 years of life and that I seemingly have a higher power looking out for me or I'm living the life of the charmed. Maybe they're one and the same. Since I don't subscribe to a higher power I will simply encourage you to decide.

After the fifth assassination attempt on my life my dad apparently caught on to the biological mother's mental disposition. He shipped me to my grandparents (his parents) house near the Upper Peninsula of Michigan where I remained for just under the first five years of my life. He initiated a divorce. He fought for, and won custody of me. It is at this moment I must pause, Dear Reader, so that you may understand that this all occurred in the late 1970s early 1980s and that during this period of time, it was in fact, a very rare situation that a working, what would become a single dad, would retain custody of a child while still in his early years. I am forever grateful that I was removed from the situation and that my very first memories are mostly of my grandparents and that those are mostly fond. Mostly.

In his fighting to ensure I had a chance in this life, I can affirm, my dad was not an asshole.

Retaining custody of me came with a great price to my dad. In my early twenties I grew curious regarding the circumstances surrounding my biological mother and their divorce and pushed my dad to answer some difficult questions.

He was uncomfortable. He poured himself a Jack on-the-rocks, poured me one, put a lit cigar in his mouth, and sat quietly for a long time. To a twenty-something, new-to-the-real-world, impatient kid like myself, it felt like an eternity. I did have the presence of mind to sit quietly, sip my beverage, and wait. I could tell in those moments he was organizing and categorizing his thoughts. I could tell he wanted to be careful with what he said but mostly with what he was going to leave unsaid. It had been years since he put any real thought into these matters and now here was his only child asking the inevitable questions. He knew this day would arrive but he didn't anticipate *it would be like this*.

Here is what he told me:

I want you to just listen to me, Gavi.

Gavi, it was a long time ago and I am a different man now. That event changed who I was and who I was going to be. It's no small feat to become divorced from someone. There's bank accounts, maybe a house, there might be a child or children, maybe a fucking pet, cars; all of the things that are joined together to make a life become pulled apart.

Anyway, you make sure, in your life, when you think you're ready to take that step, when you're ready to get married, you make sure you're really sure. You make sure you *know* that person. You make sure you get to know their family. You had better be in love with their family just as much as you love her. Don't go off all half-cocked when *that* decision is made. You'll be a god damned chump if you do. Learn from me. Do the Donato namesake proud.

So. The matter at hand. You're interested in knowing more about your *mother*. Here's what I will tell you. Shortly after you were born, your mother went into a deep depression. She showed no signs of this when we were dating. I could tell something was off with her family, but I was young and dumb. I thought, you don't marry the family, you marry the woman. Learn from me. You *do* marry the family! Don't forget it!

I tried to discuss her condition with her but you don't *discuss* anything with *crazy*. There was no reaching her so I sent you to your grandparents. Gavi, listen to me, I kidnapped you. For a while, no one, not your mother, my coworkers, nor the lawyers knew where I had sent you; they only knew you were safe and protected. Later, I learned I probably saved your life by doing so. And later, I had to report where you were to save my ass from going to jail. I also learned that your mother figured out where you were but I think you already know that story. Do you?

He didn't give me a chance to respond, looked me over for any bodily acknowledgement and continued.

Your mother went to an institution and was later placed into guardianship. We divorced.

He paused. I think he was trying to recall the questions I had asked and he begrudgingly finished the story.

The divorce. The lawyers and your mother cleaned out my life-savings. I walked away from a house. To this day, that has never come back to haunt me and I thank God for that every day. I incurred a great deal of debt in order to survive and to ensure you were going to be protected in this life. And I had to fucking work the whole time. Meanwhile, in order to see you every once in a while I had to travel five hours up north to the U.P. It was the hardest time of my life.

But then the real slap in the face came, thank you 1980s and thank you court system. Fucking Judge and Lawyers. In order to retain sole custody of you, I was forever burdened with paying for your mother's medical insurance and medical bills. That's right! For the rest of her worthless life, I get to pay to keep her healthy and alive.

Of course, if she had lucid moments, she was permitted visiting rights. You were allowed to stay with her so long as the guardian was also in tow. Years later, when you went into the military and were legally on your own and technically an adult, I tried to fight it. I rehired the original lawyer and we all went to court. *That was a great, god damned day.* I tried to get rid of the burden of paying your mother's medical bills, which are numerous, I can assure you, but with no luck. The courts just didn't see it my way and ruled in favor of your mother. Your stepmother and I will pay these bills until she dies; may God take her life early.

He drew on the cigar thinking about what else should be said, exhaled, and swallowed the remainder of his Jack and then said:

And the rest, I think you know, and if you don't, it's history.

He was angry and flushed in the face. He was exhausted and exhaled a deep sigh. We sat in silence, he puffing on the cigar, and us both holding onto our empty glasses. We were outside and the sun was setting and we were staring off into an unfocused horizon. Then the stepmother announced from an open window that it was time for dinner. We stood up from our chairs, and walked inside. We didn't and haven't ever discussed it since.

The rest *was* history.

Most of my first memories as a toddler aren't really memories but instead are feelings. I remember feeling warm and loved by my grandma who I think of more as my mom. By the way, she feels this way too and takes any opportunity she can to let my stepmother know that grandma is the *real* mother. It is truly awesome to witness the exchange between them. And in a tangent version of this story, all of grandma's biological children were in a divorce all at the same time. All of the grandchildren ended up at grandma and grandpa's house during the divorce proceedings and all of us were not really old enough to understand what was happening. But it didn't matter then. We were loved and cared for by grandma and grandpa and we had each other. We all thought we were brothers and sisters and didn't understand until much later that we were just cousins.

Chapter 2

My biological mother did eventually realize where my dad had sent me, knew where the place was, and absent of her guardian unexpectedly showed up there. My grandma, the loving and patient woman that she is, welcomed her into the house with open arms. Couples that have been together for a great many years have telepathic communication queues and gestures that only they are cognizant of. Grandma sent grandpa an 'oh shit' queue and he reacted accordingly. What happened next remains with me to this day even though it is some thirty three years later.

I was sitting in the living room with my cousins and we were playing matchbox cars or legos or something. I remember seeing my *mom* walk through the door. I remember joyfully proclaiming, "Hey! My mom's here!"

At first, the voices were calm.

I'm here to see my son.

He's playing in the living room. You're welcome to look at him. Look, see there he is.

Grandma pointed to me. My mom looked me dead in the eye and I swear I can remember there was no smile there, only darkness. Perhaps, possessiveness. Grandpa, reacting to the telepathy, quickly collected the cousins who were obliviously playing around me and he swiftly chaperoned them to the playroom. In his mind he was already calling the police but in actuality he only called my dad. He stayed there in the playroom with my cousins.

There was a tension filling the room and the voices were slightly louder.

I know what you've done and what you're doing. I'm taking my son with me. He's mine.

I'm his mother now. You're not taking him anywhere. You had your chance. You tried to hurt him. You tried to take his life. You're no mother.

Then grandma swore at my mother in a different language as she is known to do when she is upset. Then there was silence. There were just two women in a room locked in a stare each waiting for the other to make the next move. Grandma stood with her arms folded across her chest. She was not budging. My mother was just standing there blankly. I can speculate from memory that it was though my grandma's words had not yet registered. The synapses of my mother's brain were not firing correctly that day. And suddenly…

You god damned fucking bitch! I'll kill you! I'll fucking kill you! You will give him to me right now or I swear to God! He is not yours; he is MINE! ALL MINE! I'm taking him over your god damned dead body!

I was scared. I mean, I was *really* scared. First, I had never heard these profane words before. 'Fucking, bitch, god damned', were all new terms; what did they mean? Second, I had never heard the tone before and it frightened me and froze me in place. I sat staring with wide, unblinking eyes.

My mother then, with a blood-curdling scream, bull-rushed my grandma. She was surprisingly swift for her size and my grandma was caught off guard. She was unable to react in time and perhaps could not believe this was happening. My mother, with her fake, Lee press-on nails, (I remember them being a bright red) clawed my grandma's face from forehead to chin removing four finger-width lines of flesh on each side and leaving one of the nails detached from a finger but attached to a face. A moment passed, and then for the first time, at 3 or 4 years young, I saw human blood.

Grandma was screaming and held her hands to her face presumptively looking for relief from them. Grandpa, an avid hunter, sprang into the room with a rifle or a shotgun and said very calmly:

You better god damned leave right now if you value living.

She left.

I was too young to remember what happened next and in all the years after, it has been one of those family events that no one dares to bring up. I hazily remember a sitter arriving shortly after and I can only assume that my grandpa took my grandma to the hospital. Roughly 6 hours later my dad walked through the door, scooped me up in his arms, and held me close and tight and simply whispered, "I love you, son".

I can only imagine what it felt like for him to drive 5 hours up north. There were car phones by then but we didn't have one. There were no affordable cell phones. There was no way to be in touch to know that his only son was safe. There was just the quiet hum of the tires on the highway and the increasing numbers on the mile markers.

I love you too, dad. And as my dad said, the rest *was* history. It was his history. It became part of mine.

That day we were sitting, smoking, and drinking, he didn't actually answer my questions which were perhaps too pointed but he said all I needed to hear regardless. He was right. I knew the rest of the story, at least that which was important to remember. I suspect, and due to no fault of my own, this life event of his, the actions leading to the divorce, is the fundamental reason, the root cause and perhaps the spring board, to becoming an asshole.

In that perspective, I understand and I do my best to stop pointing the finger but it does not stop me from telling this story. Should the child have to endure the repercussions of the life events of the parents? Perhaps, but I suspect it's mostly a result of proximity and not so much a result of intentional actions or decisions. But alas, I have a stepmother, and if "asshole" doesn't make it's way into the title somehow to describe her, then perhaps The Editor will find a clever way to fit it in the preface!

Chapter 3

I guess life for my dad wasn't a complete wash even if by his admission this was the most difficult period of his life. Before the divorce was final, my dad had started dating. I was still living with my grandparents at the time. One day, my dad showed up at the grandparents' home in his brand new 1982 Ford Escort and announced it was time for me to come home. I remember feeling excited that I was going to be spending time with my dad again. We'll play catch, and legos, solve puzzles, and eat candy. Oh, the mind of the still innocent. Little did I know.

I don't remember saying goodbye to grandma or grandpa or my cousins. I don't remember the drive "home". I don't remember unpacking or walking into the new house. What I do remember next is meeting my dad's girlfriend for the first time.

"Gavi? You want to go bowling with me tonight?" Of course I did. "Tonight, I want you to meet someone very special to Daddy". I asked who, but he only reiterated, "someone special". I was excited. Bowling with my dad plus meeting someone special! I couldn't wait.

We arrived at the bowling alley, set up our lanes, ordered pizzas and pop and life was still perfect. And based on my immature perception, I suddenly realized there was a strange woman sitting with us; sitting at *our* table. "Gavino, I'd like you to meet that special person that Daddy was telling you about. This…is my girlfriend." I had been raised correctly by my Grandma to "always be a gentleman, Gavi" so I stuck out my right hand for a handshake and I simply said, "Hi. My name is Gavino. It is very nice to meet you". I was so cute.

She stuck out her hand until it enveloped mine, and squeezed my hand hard returning the greeting. And just like that, I was uncomfortable. My dad was with another woman. I was just too young to really comprehend what it meant. I also didn't like the way she looked, how hard she had squeezed my hand (it hurt) or the way she was looking at me. Later, I would come to realize what that look in the backs of her eyes was.

She looked so different than my grandma and my biological mother. Grandma was a short, Italian, former beauty, with long, dark hair and dark eyes and olive skin. My biological mother was also short, with long, dark hair and dark eyes and her skin

21

darkened in the sun. This lady, this *girlfriend*, was noticeably taller than my dad, had short, yellowish curly or permed hair with light blue eyes and was as white as medieval prisoner being released from a dungeon.

What really stuck out to me more than anything was her build. She was built exactly like her father with broad shoulders (broader than my dad's), and large bones in her appendages (larger than my dad's). Although this is a different part of the story, she would later tell me and my future wife, that the reason she could not wear a sleeveless dress to our wedding, was that she had "extra bones in her shoulders". Anyway, I also remember her makeup. Her cheeks were unusually flushed due to multiple layers of unblended blush. And her eye-lids were painted blue; nearly the same color as her eyes where from quite some distance, you thought you were looking at the largest eyes in the history of Homo sapiens. Her lips were glossy bubble-gum pink. This is terrible of me to say, but her normal application of makeup was quite similar to that of a clown minus the big, red, squeaky, toy nose.

Other than the initial introduction, here's what I remember about that event. There was cigarette smoke billowing everywhere. It was noisy due to the thunderous collisions between the ball to the floor and then the ball to the pins. I was sitting on my dad's lap and he handed me a Coke, and right in front of her, asked me what

I thought. I looked at him. I then looked at her. I don't know what he was expecting me to say and I really didn't have any thoughts at the moment other than stuffing my face with pizza, drinking my pop, and throwing a heavy ball down the lane. I reached for my pop and accidentally tipped it over. The pop emptied from the glass onto the table, onto the pizza, all over me, and consequently all over my dad. He lifted me off of us lap simultaneously yelling, "God damn it, Gavi!" And then *she* spoke:

What's wrong with you!?!!? Don't you know how much that just cost your father?

I was dumbfounded. I couldn't think of anything to say or do. I finally mustered some words.

I didn't mean it. I'm sorry.

You certainly will be. Who do you think you are? Things cost money. We're trying to have a nice time here. You just hurt my feelings and you've ruined our date!

I had no reply. At 4 or 5 years old, what was I expected to say? I had already apologized. I certainly hadn't meant to hurt anyone and how exactly was *she* hurt? It's a mystery to me even in my adulthood but this was the start of a pattern that would continue and actually, still does continue to this day.

My dad finally calmed down, and said, "It's really not that big a deal, Gavino. It will dry in a few minutes. Let's go get us some more pop. Come on".

True dad. It really wasn't a big deal, and years later I can now ask the question: Were you also blind to what was just said to me by *her*? *She's* not my mom. This also was the start of a pattern for my father that in my view, still continues today – Asshole.

While I was at my grandparents, in parallel to the separation and divorce from my biological mother, my dad had been dating what eventually came to be my stepmother for a little over six months. They met on a weekend at a golf course during some kind of single's event, or church league event and to this day, my perception tells me that golf really is one of the only things they have in common other than a physiological need for oxygen.

The stepmother came from humble beginnings. Both of her parents emigrated from Germany and somehow settled in Mt. Clemens, Michigan. There is a long, sordid story somewhere between emigration and settling in the Midwest, but it is and has become lost to history.

Her father was an outstanding athlete in both bowling and baseball. However, his father would not permit a son of his to be a professional baseball player or bowler and thus the family was forever doomed to live meagerly. As the story goes, her father could have played for the Detroit, Tigers – "he was that good!" He completed schooling only up to the sixth grade and after sixth grade helped his father run a farm. When he moved off of the farm (down the road a little yonder), he landed a job working the night shift at Mt. Clemens Pottery Company. For the rest of his employable and miserable life, he came home, ate, prayed, drank Schlitz in excess, verbally abused his three daughters and one son, went to bed, and dreamt about what could have been. Lather, rinse, and repeat for fifty-plus years. On the weekends, he would play Euchre with his brothers and extended family, and from what I could tell growing up, it was the only pure joy he had in his life.

He sat in a rocker. He drank Schlitz. He played Euchre. I can't remember one single word he ever said. I can't remember any activity he ever did other than walking from the rocker to the fridge, grabbing a Schlitz, then back to the rocker, and changing the channel on the TV. He liked three shows and nothing else existed. Highway to Heaven, Detroit Tiger baseball, and Lawrence Welk. The only sounds I remember him making were the violent eructing from the nasty Schlitz. And eventually, after supporting his family for his entire life, he retired, lived off of social security and money stuffed in decaying mattresses, and then died slowly and painfully of bladder cancer.

My stepmother's mother on the other hand was made of sugar and spice and everything nice. Truly, she was a sweetheart and I cried when she died. She wholeheartedly believed in God the Father, God the Son, and God the Holy Ghost and instilled this in her three daughters and one son to a fault. She made all attempts to instill this in her grandchildren as well, but already having a grandma, who had convinced me Jesus could be found under a rock, I rebelled and resisted this influence. Anyway, she, like her husband, graduated school at a grade level of six. Ignorance is bliss as they say, and she was happy to be a stay-at-home wife raising the four children while her husband killed himself on the night shift. She kept a tidy home and believed that, other than God, family was the number one priority. My favorite memory of her was her jam-covered pancakes that she would make for me every time I came over. They were absolutely delicious and even today, if I have pancakes, I will cover them in jam and think of her.

In her life, she birthed three daughters and one son. The oldest daughter divorced herself from the family when she turned 20, moved out west, and as far as anyone knows, has lived there happily ever after. In fact, she did not even attempt a trip home at the news of either of her parents dying. The second oldest daughter still lives in Mt. Clemens, in fact, in the house that her parents raised her in, married an auto-plant worker slash gambler, and garnered a great deal of wealth from the numerous personal injury lawsuits she's filed and won. The only son was a diabetic, was handy with tools, was an Elder in the church, never left the nest, and died a virgin at the age 50 due to complications with his diabetes. Then there was my stepmother; the youngest of them all with a solid 15 years between her and the next oldest daughter. She was so young by comparison, in fact, that the second oldest daughter used to complain about having to take her on her dates. Daughters in this house were not allowed to date until nearly ready to leave the home!

My step-grandmother (hey, how am I supposed to keep them differentiated?) used to say that the birth of my stepmother "was a miracle". My step-grandma was suffering from rheumatoid arthritis prior to the birth of my stepmother. It was debilitating to the point that step-grandma was bedridden. This must have been some kind of turn-on for my step-grandpa, because, as the story goes, suddenly she was pregnant (*low and behold!*). And then, *the miracle of all miracles*, the rheumatoid arthritis completely went away upon my stepmother's birth – *thank God; all of our prayers have been answered!* – For my step-grandpa, I can only imagine his thoughts. The children were nearly on their way to becoming their own adults (except the son) and moving out (except the son), and now, there were at least 18 more years of child rearing. 'Bring me a god-damned Schlitz' was probably the primary thought.

Late in her life, the step-grandma became diabetic, developed congestive heart failure, and suffered from Parkinson's disease. Due to agitated hands from Parkinson's disease, I used to help her administer her insulin through intramuscular injections. I was very good at it. One day she was rushed to the hospital for chest pains. She came home two weeks later after having a triple bypass surgery. I helped her through this as well.

I was one of the few members of the family that was not squeamish around blood or wounds. Perhaps, the site of human blood at 3 or 4 years old inoculated me against any self-imposed perceived eeriness. I remember, back in those days anyway, that sterile ropes, for lack of a better term, would be inserted into the wound from where they removed veins to attach to the heart to bypass the clogged artery. It was my job to remove the bandage, then remove the rope from the wound, then reinsert a new, sterile rope, and then bandage. Thinking back on it, it was absolutely disgusting and no job for a seven-year-old, but like I said, I didn't seem to mind; I was helping. For a few weeks this went on. I would remove the bandages from my step-grandma's legs, sterilize with iodine, remove the long ropes from where her veins used to be, insert new ropes, then bandage the areas. She was tough and I don't ever remember her shying away from the pain or flinching. She always thanked me for my attention to detail and right after would give me permission to grab a pop from the fridge.

Shortly after her bypass, while entering church, she slipped, fell, and broke her hip. She never recovered. I was a pall bearer in her funeral. I loved both of my grandma's very much. But back to her children…

All of the step-grandparent's children were raised in a devout manner in the tenets of Lutheranism, Missouri Synod branch. They all attended Sunday school, went to church on Wednesdays and Sundays, went to an attached private Lutheran school (grades 1 – 8), were baptized and communed. The children sang in the choir. The son was an acolyte. And the parents were just so proud of their Christian upbringing. All of the children completed their schooling through high school and nothing more.

My stepmom was not very good in school. She was a C or D student at best and just barely able to finish grade school and later when she entered the public school system for high-school, almost did not finish that either. Later in her life, and early in mine, she would tell me how all of the children would make fun of her. They would call her "dumb" and "stupid" and a "retard". I don't remember how this made me feel, except glad that I was none of those. She herself would tell me, that she was "slow" and had a "learning disability". "They hurt me, just like my dad did, all of the time". I tried to dive deeper into this story but she simply didn't (still doesn't) have the vocabulary to articulate it. The take home

29

message is that she didn't have any friends and her father and her classmates thought she was mentally retarded.

Just like her father though, she excelled in sports. She would be proud to tell you that she was known as a Tom-Boy. She excelled in all of the sports available to a 1950s – 1960s school girl. She was an excellent softball infielder. She was a bulls-eye shot in archery but she hated guns. And later in life, she became really talented at golf, beating my dad on many occasions, as she liked to brag, "from the Men's Tees!" She was also one to say that if you didn't drive the ball past the women's tees, then "you'd have to whip it out". Yep.

When she completed high school she somehow found work at a local bank as an accountant. She was not very keen on anyone telling her that there was a different way to do things or more than one right answer or more than one way to do the work. Her boss was just such a person to let her know that she (the boss) wanted something completed a very specific way, her way, and not the way the stepmother was doing the job. They got into a direct confrontation, in which, my stepmother's *feelings were hurt*. Since the boss did not apologize for hurting her feelings, in my stepmother's view, that boss was no one she could work for any longer because, you know, "she hurt me". It was shortly after this one event that my dad married this woman. Shortly after the marriage event, my stepmother convinced my dad that her boss was an asshole and also convinced him that she should be a housewife. I still wonder if that was part of the original deal. Anyway, he agreed to those terms and my stepmother quit the only "real" job she would ever hold.

In my stepmother's spare time, she would rehearse in the choir with her baritone, cookie-monster voice, tend the garden, and keep up with both the inside and outside house chores. She kept my dad's clothes laundered, shirts ironed, made his breakfast, lunch, and dinner, did all of the grocery shopping, and etc and etc and etc. She completed all of the tasks that a good, little housewife should complete. To make a little extra money for the house, she would cut the grass of all of the older ladies who belonged to the church and who no longer had husbands or sons to help.

She also had a side "business", she inherited from her mother when she died. She would sell Stanley Home Products. Stanley Home Products are meagerly priced cleaning products for the home or business and are manufactured by the Fuller Brush Company in Kansas. I don't know if this side business ever really made her any money, but it was a perfect fit for her. She didn't have to do any research on how to do it because all of her customers were inherited. All of the products, the forms, and the business model were also inherited. In the end, my stepmom gave this business up before I moved out of the house. 1. It was too much work; it was hard. 2. All of the clients were old and eventually all died off leaving no one left, in her mind, to sell too. Sometimes, when I visit, I will go into the basement and see if there are any Stanley Home Products left on the shelves. There always are; they are left over, forgotten, expired, and useless inventory.

The stepmother was also apparently good at accounting even if it had to be performed her way. She helped one local restaurant with "the books" and in doing so made a few extra dollars. Other than that, she was in charge of my dad's money and the budget. Growing up, I remember many occasions where this was a point of contention in the marriage.

I'll be going out for lunch today with some work colleagues and I need at least forty bucks.

You have twenty for the week. The budget doesn't allow you to have any more than that. You are not allowed any more than that.

Excuse me!? I make the money, and damn good money too. If I need more, I'll god damned take more. Sheesh! What the hell!? I can't have forty dollars for lunch!? That'll be the day!

I'm just saying. We won't be able to go out to eat on Friday if you take forty now for lunch. I don't get to go out to lunch. I have to stay here at home, taking care of Gavi and the house.

Gavi's in school. What's there to take care of in the house? The house is clean! For Christ's sake! I don't need this, this morning. I'm taking forty dollars. I'm going to have myself a nice lunch. You have yourself a nice day now. And later, if I want more money, I'll god damned take more money. I work hard for it and you don't control me! You're not my mother!

I can't talk to you right now. You're hurting my feelings.

Hopefully, by now Dear Reader, you can see the pattern.

Chapter 4

For the first five years of my life, I was raised by my grandma and grandpa and intermittently saw my dad. My biological parents divorced. My biological mother went insane but not so much that she wasn't permitted rights to see me or have me visit her. My dad remarried an uneducated, religious, homebody who apparently also was in charge of his money (Yeah, that makes sense). Yet, she was slow, or had a learning disability, and went around claiming how everyone was hurting her all the time. And then there's me; in the middle. Too young to understand everything but old enough to understand some things. Old enough to realize that there was tragedy occurring all around.

I think it's time to reiterate the point of this story. Doyoung and I are seriously considering the prospect of bringing new life into this world. We are sound from a financial perspective. We are each gainfully employed in industries and careers that we love and are successful in. We are each in our thirties and honestly feel like the timing is perfect. At the same time, Doyoung and I have similar upbringings and we feel a bit tormented, so is it worth it?

My initial perception and my retrospective review of my-so-called-life-events is that my parents were assholes. They back up this perception by reminding me in many conversations that "we are not assholes or something". They were selfish and militaristic and were frugal in my upbringing. They would say different, and probably will when this work is published. And that is exactly my intent. And you can judge for yourself. Are my extremely conservative-republican, retired, stay-in-one-place parents, assholes?

My true hope is that I can rebuild a floundering relationship with my dad and to learn something about myself along the way. To create a dialogue. I have not yet done a very good job at explaining who my stepmother is, but she is very much disliked by the immediate family, has been mostly disowned by her blood-family, and has very few friends. My dad, in recent years, since his retirement really, has taken on many of her attributes. He suddenly has low to no sense of urgency, drinks and naps all of the time, is growing morbidly obese, and where we used to have a lot in common, I find it more difficult than ever to speak to him on common ground.

An additional hope for this story is to really try to understand where I come from to help develop who I want to be as a father if or when that time comes. I hope this will help me understand me better. I have demons from my upbringing and lately they are surfacing. I do not want to pass on my demons or my perceived parental bad habits. I know Doyoung does not want this either. My hope is that the journey brings comfort and peace and, in a way, prepare me for that which I do not yet understand. We'll see.

In any event this is going to be difficult to translate to the black and white.

Here's a discussion we had recently:

Hey dad, it's Gavi. How's it going?

Hey Gavi. Good, how are you?

Good. Hey do you have a few minutes, like maybe 15 or so?

Sure. Shoot. What cha got?

Well, I thought you and mom would be interested to know, that Doyoung and I are getting ready to consider having a baby. Now, before you say anything, this is just something we are considering but are not yet actively pursuing. Er, we're active, but, you know what I mean.

Ok. Great. Is that all you wanted to talk about?

No. Give me a second. Okay. Well, you know Doyoung and I. We like to have a plan. I know what you're thinking, dad, that we can't plan out everything, but planning has worked out for us so far so just hear me out for a second. Okay, we like to have a plan. We have been in deep discussions about parenting styles. We've seen each other's parenting style while raising T'Pol and for the most part, we each like what we see of the other. Doyoung and I have also been discussing our individual upbringings. We each have been discussing certain memories and how our parents have reacted to certain situations and have basically been evaluating what our approach would be, if we, as parents were put in a similar situation. Sound good so far?

Yeah. This is an interesting approach.

Okay. So, with that in mind, and if it's okay with you and mom, I'd like to start calling home more often. Maybe take up an hour or so of your time and have you relive some old memories with me. You know, to understand your perspectives and if possible, to tell me why you think you made decisions the way you did. To tell me why you thought it was the right decision given what you knew at the time. I don't know dad, but I bet we each surprise each other by this dialogue. So, what do you think?

Yeah, that sounds great, Gavi. It will be nice to have you calling home more often for sure.

Dad, I call at least once a month. Do you want to talk more often? All you have to do is pick up the phone and...

And now an example with *her*

Hey mom, did dad tell you about our last conversation and what I'd like to do?

With disdain...

No. You're father doesn't tell me anything.

In an unsupportive voice...

What is it you want to do now, Gavi?

37

Like, what I've done to this point in my life has caused you any harm or grief. I will tell you more about this, Dear Reader, a little later.

Oh. It's a really good thing. I'd like to call home more and

Interrupting me mid sentence...

That's good Gavi. You never call home and you haven't been home for the holidays in years.

I was just there in October. Right. I don't come home for the holidays for reasons you're well aware of. Should I remind you of those reasons? I call home once a month. You have three phones in the house, and two of them are mobile, why don't you pick up the phone and dial my number if you want to talk? (silence) That's what I thought. Anyway, I'm going to be calling home more often because Doyoung and I are thinking about having a baby soon and Interrupting me mid sentence again...

Out in California, Gavi?

Yes. This is where we live. This is where our careers are.

You're the only ones out there you know!

Yes. I know. This is where we live. This is where our careers are. There is nowhere in Michigan where I can be sure my career

38

will thrive; we already tried that. The reason we are in California is because of Michigan's economy where one month after we were married, Doyoung was laid off by her firm. Anyway! We are planning on trying for a baby soon, and I'd like to talk to you and dad about how I was raised. I'll have some very specific questions based on what I can remember and all I'm hoping for is your opinion of each thing that I can remember. I will want to ask some questions but I'm not trying to be confrontational or argumentative. I'm doing this so that I can be a good dad. How does that sound to you?

How do you expect us to see our grandchild all the way in California?

You're retired. You have an RV. How about driving across the country? You know what? Put dad back on the phone. Hey dad. So, I'd like mom to be involved in what we just talked about. Can you explain it to her?

Yes, Gavi. I'll explain it to her.

Great dad. Love you. Gotta run.

Love you too. Tell Doyoung I said "Hi" and "good luck with the baby making. Have fun!"

Come on dad.

In reality, many of the conversations with my stepmom go exactly like that except with more sarcasm and general disapproval from her. And why the disapproval? Because it's not how she would have done it. I'm being serious. It is really quite trying.

Chapter 5

It's funny and maybe somewhat disturbing what the mind of a little child can retain for later recall. I mean, at least it's mostly funny to me what I can remember. I can recall tagging along on some dates with my dad and his new girlfriend. I mean right away, as I write that, I'm thinking, 'come on dad, get a damn sitter'. I can recall going to the movies with them and sitting on the opposite side of my dad away from the girlfriend. On one date we went and saw Escape from New York. Probably not the best movie for a traumatized kid to watch, but I was just happy to be hanging out with my dad, eating popcorn, and drinking pop. I remember that I could mostly understand what was going on in the movie and how cool Snake's eye patch was, but more than anything, I remember being extremely careful about how I handled the popcorn and the pop so as not to spill any of it. I remember that *she* would periodically glance my way, through my father, so that *she* could be sure I wasn't doing anything *she* felt I wasn't supposed to. I didn't want *her* to scold me, I didn't want to hurt *her*, but most of all, I didn't want to worry about my dad having to spend any more money than was necessary and all I really wanted to know was that I was being a good boy.

One time, after a date, we went back to her place. She owned a nice townhome in downtown Mt. Clemens and during this time she was still working for the bank. She owned one of the coolest things I had ever seen in my life. It would be considered retro now, but she had a hanging, mineral rain oil lamp. For those who might not remember what these are, take a moment to Google image – 1970s Mineral Rain Oil Lamps. You can buy these on eBay these days if you think they're cool. I still think they're cool but I don't think Doyoung is too impressed so I won't be picking one up anytime soon. Anyway, we came back from the date, and she turned it on for me. It was lighted and the oil recycled itself through the pan and drizzled like rain on the cords, trapping yet silhouetting the Greek goddess in the middle. I could stare at it for hours. It was calming.

The townhome was nice enough and was made up of two levels, but it was small. It had all of the essentials for a single woman who recently had moved out of the nest and was barely on her own for the first time. It had one bedroom. From what I recall, it also only had one bathroom, on the upper level, connected to the one bedroom.

One thing led to another that night and it was decided that we were staying the night. I remember being handed some pillows and some blankets and was told that I would be sleeping on the floor. I don't think I minded. Then the girlfriend handed me the largest teddy bear I had ever seen. It was larger than me. She said, "Gavi, you can snuggle with Teddy tonight, if you want, to keep you warm and to scare off the monsters." "Monsters!? You have monsters, here?!" Now I was scared. I'm in a strange place for the first time, having to sleep on a stranger's floor, and apparently, the place was going to be cold and filled with monsters. My dad reassured me there were no monsters and he cast one of those glances to *her*. You know the kind, like, 'why would you say something like that to him; I thought you wanted to get it on'.

I felt reassured by my father's words and started to assemble my sheets, blankets, and pillows in my designated, carpeted floor-bed. I brought the humongous teddy bear to the designated spot and laid him down next to me. Although the bear was cute, it did have a disturbing look to it. It had humongous plastic eyes, the kind that circle around each other when the bear is jarred. It was mostly dark brown, but the face and stomach were vanilla. Its nose was black and it had a giant, red, flapping tongue protruding from its face. The girlfriend told me that Teddy was very special to her. That he had been a gift from her great-grandma, and that this was the one item she owned from great-grandma that helped the girlfriend remember her, *and* that "[I] had better not do anything to damage him". My dad and his girlfriend, peered down at me from the second level hallway, felt confident and comfortable that I would be okay by myself and made their way to the bedroom.

Shortly after I had lain down, as anyone with young children might predict, I had the urge to go to the bathroom. I drank a lot of pop at the movies and between the excitement of the movie plus the mineral rain oil lamp, I lost track and forgot to let my dad know that I needed to go. What was I going to do?

At four years old, I was already devising plans and acting on them. I knew I needed to make it up the stairs to the bathroom but I remember feeling worried that I might wake up my dad and his girlfriend. I didn't want to make anyone mad at me but at the same time, I really needed to go. It was getting so bad, I felt like I was going to burst. I started to make my way up the stairs slowly, one step at a time. At each step, I paused and listened. I was listening for any signs that I was caught. I was listening to my feet hitting the steps. I was trying to feel for any give in the step which would subsequently or most likely lead to a creak or a squeak and at feeling the slightest give, would place my foot in a different spot. I successfully made it up half of the stairs without a peep when I froze in my tracks. There were noises coming from behind the door where my dad and his girlfriend were. My first thought: Oh no! Monsters! I wanted to yell out, 'Dad, are you okay?!?' but then I remembered, my dad said there were no monsters here. So, I stood and listened for a few minutes.

There were slapping sounds. There were lip smacking sounds. Rustling sounds from sheets, blankets, and pillows. And of course, mutual, reciprocal, guttural groaning followed by mostly comprehensible words. Yes. Oh, yes. Yes! Oh, oh, oh, wait, wait, ok, ok…uh uh. Anyway, yes, they were having sex. Perhaps, there were monsters after all; the Monster With Two Backs with the colliding of their Uglies. But of course, I didn't know that's what was happening at the time. This was another scary moment for me. I needed to go to the bathroom like right now! What the heck was going on behind the closed door? No matter what my four year old imagination told me was going on, I felt it was impossible to interrupt it for the fear of being reprimanded by the girlfriend. After all, this was *her* place.

I slowly made my way back down the stairs. What was I going to do? I needed to go pee more now than ever before. I bundled the blankets and sheets into a large ball. I laid down prone in them with my crotch lined up perfectly with the bundle, held it for as long as I could, continued to listen to the strange sounds, and finally, simply.let.it.go. From my young perspective, it exited like a torrential downpour. It soaked, through and through, all of the blankets and sheets given to me. I breathed out a huge sigh of relief when I was finally empty. I had had the presence of mind to remove my pants and underwear before letting it go. I also had the presence of mind to let it go in the bundle so that I wouldn't ruin the carpet.

After I was done peeing into the blankets and sheets, I put my underwear and pants back on and piled the soaked sheets and blankets onto the tiled kitchen floor. Now I only had pillows and the teddy bear. I laid down onto the carpet, put Teddy on top of me, and tried to fall asleep. Without the blankets, I was cold, and did not immediately fall asleep. I can still remember shivering from literally being cold, but also shivering from figuratively feeling cold and ashamed of what I had just done. I didn't want to pee on the blankets or sheets. I also knew I would be in trouble in the morning for having done so.

Then, I did something to compound the situation. I started rough housing and wrestling with Teddy. I learned the art of rough housing from my older cousins while staying with my grandma. As I already told you, Dear Reader, Teddy was much bigger than me and I had no way of knowing that Teddy as a stuffed animal was 1) an antique and 2) fragile.

I started by punching Teddy in the face. I was no longer worried about waking anyone up or any of the repercussions of damaging Teddy. Although I can't tell you for sure, I believe I was pretty annoyed at the situation. Wouldn't you be? Anyway, I grabbed Teddy by the back of the head with my left hand, and started punching him in his vanilla face with my right. Blow after blow after blow for about fifty punches; it felt good and I was getting warm. Then, I grabbed him by one of his arms, somersaulted him in the air and threw him as hard as I could into the floor. He bounced a few times. I picked him up and launched him across the room into the farthest wall. He thudded against the wall, his stupid, plastic eyes circled around themselves, and then he thudded to the floor. Now he was lying comfortably on the floor so I took a few steps backward, sprinted forward and leapt feet first to dropkick him. By my imagination only he was pummeled to a pulp and lifeless, so I straddled him and rapidly punched him in the face and gut with both fists until I could punch no more. I was tired and it was dark in the room and I remember noticing raised impressions on the carpet that weren't there before. I thought, 'I'll figure out what that is later' and just like that, I drifted off to sleep still straddling Teddy.

As it is each and every day, the night gave way to the morning and the girlfriend was the first to greet me. I had exhausted myself in the ordeal of creeping up the stairs, holding my urine, figuring out where I could safely expel the urine, and the UFC match with Teddy. The girlfriend walked down the stairs at first light where she saw me still comfortably lying atop of Teddy. Then she yelled, "Oh my God! Manlio! Get down here and look what *your* son did".

I can only imagine *her* horror. I love my grandma very much. Anything she's given to me is held close to the heart. It is what I will have left when she is no longer with us. It is sentiment in its purest form. I can understand how the girlfriend would feel when she first laid eyes on a destroyed Teddy. From the face punches, I had nearly taken his head off. There was stuffing from his face and neck strewn all over the carpet from one end of the room to the other, hence the raised impressions. The seams of his abdomen burst from the drop kick and the straddling, and he was hemorrhaging stuffing. I think the worst part for the girlfriend, was that I somehow had also separated the floppy tongue from Teddy's face. It was lying lifelessly on the carpet at her feet. She had walked as far as her witless brain would allow her and she stood paralyzed by the site of the detached tongue.

This is what I remember next. She rushed over to me and grabbed me by the scruff of my shirt and buried her face into mine. She was holding me aggressively, angrily, and she looked insane. Her forehead was pressed hard against my forehead. The tip of her nose was touching the tip of mine. She was breathing out of her mouth heavily and it stank like fecal matter (probably from eating my dad's ass in the night). Her face was red (not from unblended blush). Her blue eyes were bulging and with a snarling face and a teeth-clenching, growling voice she said:

I told you. You little shit! This was really important to me. Look what you've done. You look! You'll pay for this. You better god damned believe it. Oh, you'll pay. I'll take it out of your little ass. I let you stay in my house and this how you treat me?!

And then she slapped me, twice, once on each cheek with the back of her man hand. It was not a soft slap; it was still open handed versus a fist, but with all of her extra shoulder bones it had quite a repercussive effect as my head slammed one way, then the next.

I was shaking. There was no way I could understand this. What I could understand was the hostility being unleashed on me. In the night before, I had taken great precautions not to soil my clothing so I could stay warm, and comfortable, but I was so scared by this act that I wet myself. There was no sympathy from the girlfriend and the belittling continued.

Look at you, you little baby. What...does the baby need a diaper? Aww...did you go pee pee in your pants? Gross!

49

It was about this time that she realized I had "pee peed" somewhere else; all over her blankets and sheets.

What the hell is this!? Oh my God! Manlio! Manlio! God damn it! Your son is disgusting; you didn't tell me he was a god damned bed wetter!

I finally found some words; there was also an abundance of tears, snot, and tremors.

I'm not a bed wetter! The door was closed. There were sounds. There was no bathroom! I had to go so bad. I had to go! I didn't know where to go. You didn't tell me where I could go. I didn't want to wake anyone up.

The disturbance finally brought my dad, Manlio, down the stairs. He was scratching his bald head and he had furrowed brows. He said, "What the hell is going on down here?" He looked around just as soon as he asked the question and just took it all in. I swear I remember a twinkle in his eye and a slight smirk. My dad had a really great sense of humor. He then said, "Why does it smell like piss?"

Your son wet the bed last night and destroyed Teddy. Just look! Look at the pile of pissed on linens! Teddy is dead.

Gavi, did you wet the bed last night? Be honest with me.

With some composure reinstated…

No daddy. I peed in the blankets and sheets. I had to go. The door was closed and there were sounds. I didn't know where to go. The door was closed and there were sounds!

What do you mean sounds?

I mimicked some of the sounds I heard the night before. My dad's face turned red. *She* finally understood what I meant too.

Stay here, Gavi. I'll be right back.

My dad walked away from me, grabbed the girlfriend by the arm and conferenced in the kitchen out of my earshot for a long time. I have no idea what they talked about but there were many hand gestures and raised eyebrows. What I do remember is that my dad was really calm with me. He helped me change my clothes. He picked up all of the urine-soaked sheets and blankets and started doing the laundry.

He sat me down on the couch and we discussed the matter.

Gavi, I understand what happened and daddy is not mad at you for peeing in the blankets and sheets. In fact, I think it's pretty ingenious and downright considerate that you went there, instead of the carpet.

Ingenious?

Yes Gavi, it means smart. You're a smart little boy.

I was gleaming.

But about Teddy...

I was wrestling with Teddy. It was dark. I didn't know I was hurting him. I was just playing with him.

The girlfriend was upstairs. I had no idea what she was doing but life was perfect again; for this split moment in time, it was just my dad and I.

Well Gavi, what are we going to do about Teddy. Cheryl is really upset. You know her great-grandma gave that to her right? Well, let's assess the damage and see what we can do. Also, you should probably apologize. Go and tell her you're 'sorry' okay?

Ok dad.

My dad started picking up all of the stuffing and I helped. I picked up the tongue and handed it to him with innocent looking eyes. He laughed. I knew it was all going to be okay. My dad understood what happened. He ended up taking Teddy to some shop with a nice Asian lady behind the counter. He explained it all to her and she nodded with understanding. A week later, Teddy was all better. All of the stuffing was back in place, the head was reattached, and the tongue, although slightly skewed with an off-red thread-scar, was firmly attached and floppy again. I had apologized to Cheryl but she was not yet ready to accept or forgive or forget. As I would find out later in my life, she could forgive, but she could not forget – not ever!

When Teddy was fixed my dad thought it would be a great idea if I were the one to re-present the new and maybe not so improved Teddy. I was bright-eyed with excitement at the prospect of showing the girlfriend (Cheryl) that Teddy was all better. When I gave it her, she didn't react with the same excitement.

Look Cheryl! Teddy's all fixed! See?

Great. Thanks. I hope you learned your lesson.

The excitement rushed out of me. I could tell. I had *hurt* her again.

Years later, I was on leave from the military. It was one of my first trips back home after joining the military and I was fairly excited to see friends and hang out with the parental units (my dad and the stepmother). I had a serious girlfriend at the time. She was my first "real" relationship and at 19, I thought I was in love. And by real, I mean we were doing all of the things that young, healthy, non-religious couples do (The religious ones do it too, by the way – they just don't take public credit for it). She was a few years older than I was and really showed me the ropes, physically, if you know what I'm saying. Of course, I thought this relationship would lead to marriage.

Anyway, at this point of my life I had been out on my own, in the military for almost two years. I was living in a different state and I had my own military supplied housing. I was technically an adult; free to make my own decisions for my life.

I told Cheryl that I had a girlfriend. She responded in a predictable fashion.

I hope you're keeping it in your pants. We don't want any bastard grandchildren running around. You know, you're father and I didn't have sex until we were married. I have only ever been with him and I was a virgin until my wedding night.

I stared at her with a surprised look on my face. Literally, my eyes were wide and my jaw was slack. I didn't think about my words before uttering:

You're such a liar.

It was the first time as an adult that I didn't just accept what was being said to me by a parent. It was the first time as an adult that I *really* questioned her so-called authority. Her eyes got wide as though to ask me who the hell I was. I continued as though I had not seen the look.

You don't remember do you? What you just said to me is an outright lie.

Be careful what you say to me. I'll involve your father.

Go ahead. Is he around? Let's involve him. I would really rather enjoy that, I think.

I am not lying. We didn't have a physical relationship until we were married.

You are lying. You must not remember. I was there, before you were two were married. Sleeping on your townhome floor. Remember the night I pissed all over your blankets and sheets because you guys forgot to tell me where the bathroom was? Oh yeah. Remember the destruction of Teddy? I remember. Well, I want you to know that I am NOT keeping it in my pants. We have sex. A lot of it! That's right mom, I have sex, and I'm really fucking good at it! I make her quiver after.

You better not!

I do. I'm also an adult. Recognize it. Time to loosen the grip. Besides, there is absolutely nothing you can do about it.

I had a huge smile on my face. I had caught her in a lie. My super-conservative, highly religious, bible abiding parents had sex out of wedlock and then lied to me about it. Oh, the audacity and the hypocrisy to tell me I couldn't do the same thing. Again, it's fascinating what the young mind will remember. Neither of my parents could have ever imagined I would have remembered that night and that I could associate the sounds they were making to an act of sex. She could think of nothing else to say and simply walked away. Asshole.

Shortly after the destruction and resurrection of Teddy, my dad and his girlfriend became engaged. It was a night like any other in Michigan. And other than the question and the anticipation in waiting for the answer, there was nothing else special about that event. My dad planned a simple night out to dinner for just the two of them, and during dinner he popped the question and she said yes. The end.

The wedding was to be had at the church she and all of her family were members of. I was nearly five years old. My only memory of the wedding was walking down the aisle escorting my flower-bearing cousin. I had a cute little-boy tuxedo on and as we walked down the aisle together, I remember feeling proud that in that one moment, I was the center of attention. All of the older women at the event were "ooing" and "awing" at how cute I was. The reception occurred somewhere else.

I was a hellion at the reception. I don't remember the venue, but I do remember feeling as though I was in the biggest place I had ever been in. I remember tables and chairs and people everywhere. I knew most of the people but there were many that I didn't know. I was left to my own devices which at five years old, for a little boy with a lot of physical energy and a lot of nervous energy can never be a good thing. I ran around the place, sat next to random individuals, and started punching them and kicking them for no reason. Once I felt the kicking and punching were complete, I would run off, as though I could not be caught, and found the next victim to kick and punch. I could not be controlled or consoled. My dad was made aware of the situation, found me, and spanked my ass right on the spot. I deserved it. I was being an asshole. My stepmother, and not in a joking fashion, still likes to bring up how I nearly "ruined her big day" and what a "little terror" I was.

Years later, when I introduced Doyoung to my parents for the first time, my mom brought out the wedding photo albums. For the most part, I really didn't remember looking at the pictures myself while growing up, so it was a great opportunity for Doyoung and I to review and go through whatever memories the pictures brought up. The usual memories surfaced. This is "that" person, and this person belongs to this side of the family, and oh look there's grandma and grandpa and how young everyone looks etc. When Doyoung and I were alone for the evening and saying our good nights, we both had a similar observation and remarked as such. There were very few pictures of me anywhere in the wedding. I was a ring-bearer so you'd think there would be more. You would think there would be pictures of me walking down the aisle. You would think there would be pictures of my dad and I, and then the three of us, maybe me with the extended family. There are a few like that, but the majority of purchased and printed pictures are those of her and her family. I didn't know it back then, of course, but this observation became the start of a pervading thought. Even back then, in the initial stages of the relationship, the relationship that was supposed to be the introduction of that which was to be my new mother, I was only a tertiary thought. Assholes. (And also, it's okay because I paid her back at my wedding by intentionally excluding the mother son dance).

The day after the wedding, I was baptized. I don't remember wanting to be baptized. I don't remember asking for this, rather, it's what *she* wanted. They were married in the church and by so doing my dad had become a member of the church. In the same regard, I was to now enter the church membership through baptism.

After the baptism event, my parents went on a Hawaii honeymoon and during that time I stayed with *her* parents, my grandparents-in-law. They were oh-so-proud that their youngest daughter was married in the church and that there inherited grandson was now also indoctrinated. They lived locally so it made sense to stay with them but I remember stubbornly putting up a fight to stay with my dad's parents. Afterall, my real mom, my grandma, was up north. That's who I wanted to be with but *she* was not having it. At that point in our lives, grandma despised Cheryl and told my dad that she was the wrong woman for him. Especially after the divorce event had only recently concluded with my biological mother.

When they came back from Hawaii my stepmom moved in with us and after a short time sold the townhome. I will remind you, Dear Reader, that I am barely five years old at this time. Cheryl moved in along with all of her stuff and now it was the three of us in the house. I remember being really confused. Do I now ask Cheryl for a grilled-cheese sandwich and pop? Is Cheryl cleaning the clothes? Why is Cheryl tucking me in at night?

In as best as I could, I brought this up to my dad.

Dad. What do I call Cheryl?

She's your mom now, Gavi. You will call her 'mom'.

But she's not my mom.

He sat me down on the couch. I'm not sure if he had thought about this. I suppose in his mind he figured it was the natural thing to do. In his mind, it was totally appropriate to call two women, 'mom'.

Well, Gavi. I'm sure Cheryl will really like it if you called her 'mom'. You don't want to hurt her feelings do you? Try, 'mom' on for size for a while. I mean it, you call her 'mom' for just a little while. And later, if you don't like it, you can change back to Cheryl.

But he knew there would be no change backs. He tricked me into calling her 'mom'. To my knowledge, he was only ever able to trick me one other time regarding finances and grandpa. Anyway, at five, I didn't want to call her 'mom'. Cheryl would have been sufficient for me. At fifty-five, I will still not want to. She called me out on this once when I was intelligent enough to understand my situation. (okay, many more times than just once). We were in some fight, as we usually were, about something she wanted me to do one way, but I refused and did it my own way.

60

You listen to your mother. What I say goes. You will do as I command because I am your *mother*.

I made no response. She could tell I was having an internal conflict.

You wish I wasn't your mother don't you? Your father married me; I'm your mom. That's life.

Yes, that is life. An imperfect one. And so they were married now. And then I had a new mom, plus a mom, plus someone I actually bonded to as a mom. Imagine being five years old trying to balance three mothers without any guidance from a risk averse harmony-loving father. I am not saying it was easy for Cheryl either. But the adults should have a better understanding of the ramifications and the delicate psyche of a little boy who was being shuffled around without an afterthought.

I have my suspicions and my speculations about why things were the way they were. I will tell them to you in good time. There were no change-backs and no matter how old she gets or I get, there will never be a change-back. I was tricked into and therefore forced to call this woman, 'mom'. It wasn't fair and it wasn't right. From my adult perspective, it is damn near evil. The rest of our small community thought it was so dear that little Gavi had taken so well to Cheryl so much so that he thought of her as his 'mom'.

The rest of the family knew better but who were they? They weren't in the circle of knowing except when they were and that was very rare. Thanksgiving? Christmas? These are mere dots in the scope and breadth of a childhood.

Grandma knew though. And grandma is all that mattered.

Chapter 6

I spent the first year of grade school, kindergarten, in the public school system. The wedding took place towards the end of the kindergarten year during the fall and my parents thought it best that I finish the year in that school. At the end of the school year though, I was informed that I would be transitioning to the private school attached to the church. We lived in a neighborhood where most of the like-aged children were attending the school system that I was going to. In other words, all of my friends attended the school that I was already at and were quite literally, my neighbors, and my neighborhood pals.

I will never forget Michelle Coel who was the same age as I was and lived three doors down. Michelle was a cute, little brunette girl with big, green eyes. We liked each other's company very much. As much as five year olds can, anyway. On cold, winter days, I would go and knock on her door and her parents would always let her come out and play with me. One day, she knocked on mine. I was so surprised, delighted really. I let her in, held her hand, and walked her to my dad for an introduction. He had a father's grin on his face at seeing all of this transpire and I'm sure we looked absolutely adorable together.

It's nice to meet you Michelle. Can I take your coat? And, would you like some hot chocolate?

Soon, Michelle and I had two marshmallow filled Nestle Quick's in our cold hands and were simultaneously blowing on them to cool them off. We were snuggled comfortably on the couch. We were two peas in a pod. We were innocent friends. I had no idea where my mom was but my dad left us alone to let us just be kids.

Michelle had a great idea. "Do you want to kiss me, Gavi?" I blushed. Of course I did. We set our hot chocolates down, put on our cold weather gear and went outside. As I am always planning and scheming, I knew, even back then, that it would be a bad thing to get caught kissing a girl and the thought was that there was no way we could get caught if we went outside.

We went to the back of the house and hunkered under one of the windows. I studied the area and decided that in this particular spot, there would be no way we could get caught. No one forgets their first real kiss. I stared into her pretty green eyes. She stared into my chocolaty brown eyes. We leaned into each other's face until our lips met, and kissed, innocently. It was the kind of kiss where the lips just barely overlap with each other and only the slightest moistness is exchanged. The kind where you can just barely catch the sweet smell of her hair and feel the slight breeze of her breath. We both enjoyed the first kiss, as much as five year olds can, so we kissed some more. We were blushing but enjoying the innocent moment for exactly what it was.

After a while, my dad caught on to the fact that he was no longer hearing noises from us in the living room. He came to check on us. He was concerned when he didn't immediately find us in the living room. He put on his coat, went outside, and before we knew it, we were caught.

Gavi! What's going on?

I turned and looked at him. Michelle went running for her life. She never even looked back! We both let her go. My dad had is arms folded across his chest. He was grinning from ear to ear and his eyes were twinkling.

What were you guys doing?

Just kissing, Daddy.

Oh yeah? Did you like it?

Yeah. Why wouldn't I like it?

Ok. Ok. Just be careful and don't let your mother know. And maybe next time, just stay in the house ok? I was really worried for a second there. I don't want to have to explain to some girl's father that I lost her on my watch. Understand Gavi?

Yes dad. I understand.

Good Gavi. You're a smart boy. I'm proud of you. Always be a gentleman.

I know Daddy. Grandma taught me to be one.

He raised an eyebrow and momentarily maintained a surprised look.

From a young boy's perspective, I was happy about three things. First, I didn't get in trouble for kissing a girl. Secondly, I enjoyed kissing the girl. And lastly, my dad and I had a secret from *her*. My dad could be a really great guy when *she* wasn't around. And for that brief moment, life was perfect.

We were renting that house in the neighborhood and with the transition from one school to the next school, we also moved to a new neighborhood in a house that my dad bought. I saw Michelle only two more times in my life, but hardly anyone else from that neighborhood ever again.

I wrestled in high school for three years, all of them on the varsity team. I was able to wrestle all three years on the varsity team only because I was willing to take on whatever weight class was available and not because of my wrestling skills. I weighed only 119 lbs and wrestled on varsity in the 126 lbs and 135 lbs weight classes. Dudes were dropping weight from 140+lbs to wrestle in those weight classes and more matches than I care to admit, I got my ass handed to me. The dudes that I was wrestling were more advanced in their training and were muscularly humongous compared to my 119 pound slender physique.

I was known for "having heart" during my matches because I absolutely refused to be pinned and I would gut it out until the final bell of the final round. Only the most superb wrestlers, the ones who usually made it to the State Championships, were able to pin me. I was proud of the fact that I had the heart and the stamina to endure the physical punishment. I was even prouder of the fact that on most occasions they had to win by points and that I accumulated a fair share of my own points. At the end of matches, there would always be that look from the opposing wrestler that said, I can't believe I couldn't pin you – *you, 119 lbs of you.*

The high school I attended was a private school and the wrestling team was a boy's only team. At one home tournament, I had qualified to wrestle varsity at the 126 pound weight class. My coach and I went over the bracket and there were two things that stood out that were disturbing to both of us. The first disturbing issue was that in round one I would be wrestling a girl. If I won the match, I would move on to the next round of the tournament. Normally, that by itself would not be disturbing, however the next match was against my own teammate who would normally wrestle in the 135 pound weight class and would frequently hand my ass back to myself during practices. I was at odds with both issues. I asked my teammates (with exception to the potential team showdown) what the hell should I do about this.

On the one hand, if I wrestled this girl and I lost, then I would lose face and credibility and seriously get made fun of. I mean, shit, you can't go around as a man and get beat by a girl in a sport of strength with all other things, including weight, being equal. On the other hand, if I wrestled this girl and I won, then I still lose because, duh, I beat a girl. Not to mention, I'm 15 or 16 and would be rubbing on, what I expected to be an attractive high school aged girl where, the both of us, are wearing nothing but a singlet.

Back then, children did not have cell phones. My parents were not attending this event but I needed to know what to do. I put some change into the pay-phone and called home. My dad answered. (thank god).

Dad. I'm in kind of a dilemma. I'm slated to wrestle a girl.

So, what's the problem?

I explained it all to him in the same fashion as I explained it you, Dear Reader focusing mostly on the lose – lose issue. He laughed really hard. I mean, a deep, guttural laugh. When he was done laughing he said this:

You gotta go out there and kick her ass. Don't think of her as a girl. Just go out there and wrestle. She's been wrestling this whole year. She weighs as much as you do, apparently, which is scary enough but don't think of your junk. You know what I'm saying? Leave your hormones out of this! Just get it done, and win.

Ok dad. But what if I lose? What if, you know, we're rubbing together and...

He laughed some more.

Then, you lose. So what? Again, don't worry about your junk. If *it* happens, we'll talk about it later.

The advice didn't really help my mindset. I talked to the coach some more and he told me to just go out there and do my best. I was excruciatingly nervous. I was going to lose either way. At some point, immediately prior to the match, I accepted my fate. I was going to lose either way, but I would give it my best effort and hopefully still literally win the match but deal with the figurative loss later.

As is the tradition, we met at the center of the mat and shook hands and wished each other 'good luck'. My mind was racing. She had long, jet-black curly hair with green eyes. She had olive skin and she smelled so good. She was 126 lbs of long, slender muscle. She looked me over sizing up the competition and there was only focus in *her* eyes. The whistle blew and she shot forward and took me down. There was a huge crowd around this particular match and they all went crazy. They were screaming and fist pumping and feet stomping. They liked what they saw of her and everyone but my team was rooting for her.

As soon as she took me down, my mindset changed. I was immediately focused and I thought, 'there is no god damned way I am being beat by this girl or by anyone today'. I stood up from the take down. She couldn't keep me on the ground. I then took her down myself, wrapped one of my legs through hers, flipped her over so that I could put her in a half-nelson, completed the half-nelson and thirty seconds later, she was pinned – match over. The crowd dissipated. We stood up, went to the center of the mat and shook hands. In that moment, I recognized her, by those green eyes. It was Michelle.

I walked with her to the stands where her team was. I sat with her for a few minutes ("always be a gentleman") and I asked her if she remembered me, or if I seemed familiar to her. She looked at me for awhile and finally, said, 'no'. I told her where I thought I recognized her and she validated the memory, but was apparently not as impressed by the memory as much as I was. Those little moments had stayed with me throughout the next 11 or 12 years and Michelle had crossed my mind on more than just a few occasions – the sweet kiss. The conversation ended with me stumbling through some goodbye. "It was nice seeing you again. Great match. Nice to talk to you". And that was the end.

The next match was against my teammate. Long story short, I won that match too. Apparently I was inspired that day and/or my teammate was having a bad day. Either way, I won in my weight class that day and for beating a girl and my teammate, I received a copper medal which I later proudly displayed on my Varsity Jacket. And all of that lose-lose business that I was so worried about never came to fruition by anyone, anywhere. I wish I could say, 'lesson learned' but I was not yet ready to acknowledge any of life's lessons or what I should be learning from them.

Our coach was apparently really concerned about having his all-boy wrestling team, in a private school have to worry about wrestling with girls. Most of the teachers at the private high school were strictly conservative and to have boys and girls wrestling against each other could only be construed as perverse. Perhaps an act leading to thoughts about fornication or the act of fornicating itself (god forbid!). He took this issue up with the school board, and nearly immediately after this event, the school instituted a new policy. Any time a teammate was slated to wrestle against a girl, the boy would have to immediately forfeit the match. I mean, we couldn't have any boys rubbing their genitalia through their singlets on the opposing girls. That would be a sin! Obviously.

A few weeks later in an away tournament, I was slated to wrestle Michelle again. I met her at the center of the mat with my warm-ups on, and in alignment with school policy, announced my forfeit. As a result, we (collective we, the team) lost the tournament. It wasn't my fault, but at the time it sure felt like it was my fault. Later in the year, at the state championships, our star wrestler, the individual who was absolutely destined to win state that year, also had to forfeit as the opposing wrestler in the first round was a girl. You know, if I was a coach, at a public school and had learned about this private school's policy on girls, I probably would have a team of back up girl wrestlers and by default, would win state every year! I'm just sayin'.

By my own admission and from my own perspective, I was a great kid. Grade school and high school classes came easy to me. I was mostly an A student with the occasional B. Both grade school and high school were private, with a Lutheran, Missouri Synod denomination. Grade school, in the private sector is grades 1 – 8;

there was no middle school. High school was grades 9 – 12. Private high school is supposed to be preparatory for college, but I don't recall feeling prepared, quite the opposite actually.

Anyway, in grade school, I excelled at all of the courses with exceptions to arts and crafts. I probably still managed at least a B- in those courses. I was fairly popular in grade school especially with the girls. For some reason, I could seem to relate to them easier and better than the boys in the grade. I was great at sports as well and in grade school played everything there was that was available. Being Italian, I matured faster than most of the boys and found myself, even as short as I was, to be one of the strongest kids in the class. I could jump higher, throw the shot-put and discus further, run faster, do more pushups and pullups, and etc and etc.

As one would expect, my parents had strict philosophies regarding my childhood upbringing. First, there's the fact that I was attending private school. It was absolutely unacceptable for me to have a grade below a B. There was no allowance as most kids had for good grades. It was simply expected. "Your job is to go to school, Gavi. I expect that you'll have good grades. And if you don't have good grades, the privileges that you currently have that keep you comfortable in my house, will be taken away. No more television. No more play time. You will be grounded until those grades come up." I was already being told what would be taken away before I had the chance to prove how well I could do. Motivation through fear. I guess that's okay but I think there are different or better approaches.

My parents felt that it was critical that I dress appropriately for private school. My school did not have a uniform policy, only that we dressed appropriately. My parents required me to wear dress pants, a dress belt, a button down shirt, with dress shoes and dress socks. Every day like this; no exceptions. On *special occasions*, I would also have to wear a tie. In this regard, I was singled out from the rest of my classmates. My classmates were wearing jeans, tennis shoes, t-shirts or Polo's or sweaters, and came to school in comfortable attire and appropriate garb for recess. When the class would go outside to play kickball, flag football, or dodge-ball, they were ready and appropriately dressed. I would play, stain my shirts and pants with grass stains, put holes in my pants sliding into bases, and ruin my dress shoes. In many cases, my shoes would come flying off of my feet while I was sprinting around and when such a thing happened, I would usually just run around in my socks wearing them out. Each day I came home with some new damage to the Sunday best dress and subsequently would get scolded for it.

My parent's perception was that my clothes were very nice and that I was a "nicely dressed little boy". However, these clothes

74

came from K-mart or some other low-end retailer (like Big-Lot). The clothes were cheaply made and were cheap to buy. Although I was popular because I was intelligent, athletic, good looking and witty, I was often made fun of because of my blue-light-special garb. This carried over into gym class. On occasion, teachers would break from the usual grind of the classroom and exercise us in the gym with some gym-hockey. There I was, little, fast Gavi, running around in Sunday best clothes, losing his shoes and putting holes in his pants. For actual gym class, I was *permitted* to wear my gym uniform. Thank goodness.

Although I say I was a good kid, I can also say that I was starved for attention. When I came home from school, I mostly kept to myself, in my room and played with my dog, my stuffed animals, or my made up games. I'm pretty sure my *parents* preferred it this way. Better to be seen and not heard if you pick up what I'm laying down. Anyway, one of my favorite made up games was what I like to call the "paper-game".

The paper game was very simple. I would take a piece of paper, wad it up into a little ball and bat it around with my hands and feet. The object of the game was to keep it from hitting the ground. I would count the number of times I hit it or kicked it into the air. My goal was to keep it in the air longer than the last time I played or for the longest hits ever. One time, I hit it and kicked it into the air greater than one thousand times. I never beat that record and eventually, for obvious reasons, I think, I grew tired of that game. On a positive note, it was a great game for my personal athletic hand to eye coordination.

Another favorite solo game I invented was Stuffed Animal Wars. I had a variety of stuffed animals and G.I. Joe's and other Lego type action figures. I would pretend that they were all against me and much like my battle with Teddy, I would dominate and destroy, in fake fist fights, each figure, one at a time.

As a result of this independency from my biological mom, my stepmom, and subsequently my dad, and in an attempt to garner some attention from classmates and teachers, I acted out in school on more than a few occasions.

In the first grade, being that it was a new school for me, completely different in almost all ways, there was no acting out. Just learning and adapting to the new environment so for that first year, I was a complete angel. The acting out started in the second grade.

In the second grade I seemed to always be in detention or made to stand in the hall. More times than not, I'm sure it was substantiated. In the private school system that I attended, and starting in the second grade, children receive "Sex Ed" or sexual education as part of the Health Curriculum.

I already felt, in the second grade, that I knew all I needed to know about Sex Ed and made light of it. I knew what a penis and vagina was. I knew that mommies and daddies got together to use those to create babies. I maybe didn't know how those things worked together, per se, but I did feel like I was knowledgeable. I felt I knew because of the life experiences I had both been surprised by and endured.

Behind our house was empty field space. In particular areas of the empty field were small patches of large trees. Some kids, older than me or my buddies, built tree forts in them. There was also a water runoff from a main road forming a make-shift ditch. One day, my buddies and I were gallivanting through the empty fields, playing our Jungle Games, when we came across a box of discarded Hustlers. These were fully intact, hot off the presses, "nudy" magazines.

My buddies and I were in heaven. At first we thought the pictures of naked ladies, fully exposed, with full vaginal frontal exposure were gross and in many ways made us feel uncomfortable or guilty. At seven or eight years old, I don't think you're intended to see or try to understand these images. However

77

after repeated visits and repeated ogling, we all grew very fond of the articles and the pictures. Anyway, those nudy magazines gave me and a bunch of friends all the sex ed we felt we needed. One day my dad asked, "What do you guys do when you go out there? You've been going out there nonstop for many many days." I couldn't think of an adequate lie so I told him the truth. I told him there were a bunch of nudy magazines left behind that we read and look at and laugh at. He was quiet for a few minutes. At first I could tell he was deeply concerned. And then, he simply said, "Ok. Just try not to get too caught up in it". Another cool moment between my dad and I. He did eventually tell *her* and it became not so cool. In fact, shortly after that, those magazines magically disappeared. Even my buddies knew what happened and our friendships became strained for a short time. Thanks Asshole (and what exactly did you protect me from?)!

In a tangent version to this section of the story, and around the same timeframe, my biological mother introduced me to sexual education in three very disturbing ways. I was visiting her at her parent's house where she lived under guardianship. We were sitting in her room. She was lying on her bed and I was just looking at her things and taking it all in. I had afterall, just arrived and this was my first time in a long time seeing her or her things. (If I recall correctly, the last time had been when she clawed my grandmother). As I've mentioned, she wasn't fully right in the brain. She invited me on to the bed and since this is my biological mom we're talking about, and at my young age, I had only innocent thoughts percolating.

Then it got weird. She took of her shirt. She had a bra on. She asked me to help her take off her bra. I was scared. But this was my mom telling me what to do. Respect your parents, always be a gentleman were thoughts and ideas circulating through my young mind. I was behind her and did as she told me. I fumbled around for a minute and she told me to, "Relax Gavi, and just focus, and undo the clasp". I undid the clasp and moved slightly backwards towards the head of the bed. With the bra being unclasped she removed it. I was so anxious I thought I was going to vomit on myself. I knew in my mind this wasn't right but I was still torn between doing what I was told to do by my parent while worrying what my other parents were going to think.

Now that her bra was off, there was just me standing on the bed behind her, while she was topless, with her arms folded across her chest. She asked me to stand in front of her. I relocated myself so that I would be standing in front of her. She then took her arms away from her chest to reveal herself to me. I didn't want to look but she made me.

Gavi. Look at me now, Gavi. See what a real woman looks like. Not like that retard your father now fucks. Do you know what fucking is, Gavi? If you're anything like your father used to be, I'm going to enjoy having your dick in me. I want your dick in my mouth. In between my tits. Inside of me. I want you to fuck me like your father used to. And if you're little carrot can cum, I want you to cum in me too. It's been so long for your mother.

Her eyes were rolling into the back of her head. I was crying. The last time I heard words like these was the last time I had seen my mom; when grandma had to go to the hospital. She then took my face, squeezed it hard, and turned my head. I had my eyes closed and she screamed at me.

Open your fucking eyes right now, god damn it! If you don't open them right now, I will take my fingers and poke them out! You will look. Oh yes, you will.

No mommy. I don't want to.I don't want to! I'll go to hell if I do. I don't want to go to hell!

She laughed hysterically. Loud cackling really. And to avoid having my eyes poked out, I opened them. And unremarkably, there were my biological mother's tits. I continued to cry until she felt I had had my fill of them. But to look, for her, apparently wasn't enough. She stripped off my t-shirt. She then forced me close to her. She held me tight so that we were embracing and it was her bare skin against my bare skin. She had her legs spread and was straddling me from the bottom. She pushed me forward while simultaneously grabbing my arms. She was stronger than me, and although I tried to pull away from her grip, she made my hands fondle her breasts. While she made me do this, her eyes rolled in the back of her head and she gasped and moaned with pleasure. She buried my face in her tits and all I could do was cry.

This went on for what felt like an infinite amount of time and became inclusive of dry humping. I was still crying and now I was crying so hard that I vomited. To this day, and although I rarely, if ever think about this memory, I believe the vomiting saved me any furthering of this act of incest.

The vomit covered my arms, hands, and some of it got onto her. She was outraged. You know, because I interrupted the moment, and killed the intimacy. She screamed out and finally, her Guardian, her mother, my grandmother, forced the bedroom door open and stood in the doorway simply bewildered. Her jaw became slack while a hand flew to her face to cover her gaping mouth. When all of the neurons finally connected in her brain, the *Guardian* ran to me, scooped me up in her arms and ran me out of the room repeating over and over, "Oh my poor child. Oh my poor child".

In instance number two and on a separate visit, my biological mom called me into the bathroom. She had just finished taking a bath. She told me to grab a towel. I grabbed one. She then stood up from the bath water, stark naked, and commanded me to dry her off. The Guardian, now having a heightened awareness to my biological mom's incestual tendencies, was able to get me out of that situation before any real damage was done. However, 1) I was forced to see her naked and 2) she later made me take a bath in her dirty bath water and proceeded to make sure I was a "good and clean little boy". That's all I have to say about that!

And finally, in another visit for my biological mother's birthday, she (or someone) hired a black, male stripper. And for 45 minutes, with several adults sitting in the audience, and not one of them the least bit uncomfortable that a 7 or 8 year old was in the audience (to include the god damned stripper) I was forced to sit through the performance, swinging black dick and balls and all. I remember him just laughing at the idea that I was in the room. "Well, as long as I get paid; what the hell do I care?"

Before we were married, I told Doyoung all of these stories and many more. She cried a lot and was furious with each one. When she recovered from the horror, she simply said, "I have no idea how you turned out the way you did. Thank god for Grandma.

And, I don't know how you didn't turn out to be gay, but I'm so thankful you were able to overcome all of this."

So anyway by the time it was time for second grade Sex Ed, I really felt like I had enough knowledge to skip it. And, for the most part, I wasn't really interested. Can you blame me?

The second grade teacher had a core curriculum to get through and I remember her being very uncomfortable with the subject matter. In second grade, we're six or seven or eight years old at most, so what do we possibly need to know about sexual education at that age? Anyway, there were very detailed anatomy books to read from. To make us, and probably herself too, more comfortable, she had the entire class sit in a circle around her as she read from the text. Occasionally, she would hold the book out to us so that we could review the pictures of the anatomical features of all of the "uglies". We would all giggle, snort, chuckle, point at, and say "eww" to the pictures, not really understanding what we were looking at. During the teacher's reading of the text she would very often, pause, for emphasis on the word she was about to read. "Inside of the woman's ---- vagina, there is something called a---- canal. And in this ---- canal". Ok? You get the point. During the long pauses, I thought it was a queue for the class to fill in the blank. So I started to try to fill in the blanks.

As little boys and girls grow up into young men and young women, their bodies start to change. Their bodies start to mature. So that you are not confused as young men and young women, it's very important to understand what these changes mean, and to be able to recognize when these changes are happening. Some of you may already be experiencing these changes.

I was hooked. Was I experiencing any of these changes? I needed to know! She went on.

For example, as a boy starts to turn into a man, hair will start to grow on his ---

Penis!?

No, Gavi. Well yes, but I was going to say hair will start to grow on his lip which is known as a moustache. Hair will also start to grow on his ---

Penis!?

Gavi! Let me finish.

The class erupted in laughter both from the teacher's frustration and from my vocalization of the word, 'penis' times two. In a frustrated tone, she went on.

Hair will also start grow on the armpits. Likewise, as little girls grow into young women hair will begin to bloom on her ----

In rapid succession.

Vagina. Vulva. Uvula.

Gavino Donato! How do you know those words?

I don't know. I just do.

Gavi. Just sit and listen quietly. And yes, hair will grow on both young men and young women's *private parts* which Gavi has so eloquently informed us. As a little boy continues to develop into a man, the scrotum will also begin to develop. The scrotum holds the ----

Balls!

That's it Gavi. Get out in the hall and stay there until I'm ready to bring you back in.

But Mrs. W, I'm just trying to help.

They are not referred to as "balls". They are testicles.

Tes-tik-ills.

At the pronunciation of the word, I erupted into hysterical laughter. I could not stop laughing. I had never heard *this* word before and I certainly had not read about "tes-tik-ills" in Hustler. I imagined the sight of my own balls while trying to pronounce "tes-tik-ills". I laughed until tears were streaming from my eyes and my abdomen hurt. Laughter to second graders is contagious and soon the whole class was laughing along with me. I was sent out to the hallway, where I continued to laugh at my new vocabulary word for balls. When I got home that day, I announced to my dad that I knew what testicles were. He did a double take and ran out of the room probably because he was laughing so hard.

In the third grade, I was largely the instigator of trouble. On one unfortunate occasion, I brought a new version of the paper game to the classroom. Our third grade teacher would frequently leave the classroom to attend to some phone call or some personal business or who knows what. It was the eighties afterall, so looking back on it now, I would tend to think his *business* was a dash or smidge of blow to get through the day!) He would let us know that he was leaving for a short while, put someone in the class in pseudo-charge, give us an assignment and attend to his *business*. When the teacher would leave the room, it was our queue to start the paper game. The paper game was ingenious. The worst that could happen from this version of the paper game would be that the teacher might catch a glimpse of a piece of paper floating to the ground. Nothing unusual about that.

This version of the paper game used a flat piece of notebook paper. Someone would rip out a piece of paper from their notebook, set it on the floor, and kick it as hard as they could. The paper would get sent up into the air from the force of the kick and, much like a paper airplane being thrown, would move diagonally through the air sauntering sideways to a new resting place. Whoever it landed next to was responsible for kicking it back in motion. It was fun; we were all into it even the class monitor.

Inevitably, the piece of paper landed next to me. I remember thinking, 'I'm going to kick the hell out of this piece of paper'. I stood up, got a running start, and set my legs in motion for the forceful kick. I kicked the piece of paper, but with the kick, my untied dress shoe went flying off of my foot and headed, with great speed and power, directly towards the classroom's old, drop down fluorescent lights. The shoe hit the light guard in exactly the right spot causing it to shatter and shower glass shards onto the students sitting below it. One of the shards was a one-foot piece of pointed glass. As soon as this section detached from the light, it fell like an arrow, point first, and landed, point first, piercing the top of a classmates head. It stuck there, in her head, straight up and down, for a few seconds, before gravity took over, causing the glass shard to break off and fall to the floor leaving the tip still stuck in her skull.

I am one of those strange individuals where, when something traumatic happens to someone else, and I also happen to be a witness, I laugh uncontrollably. This is not just a short, chuckling kind of laugh. This is an uncontrollable, hysterical, laugh until I cry kind. It's always been this way for me and only a very few people understand it. It's a sign of a psychopath. Just kidding, it's a stress induced coping mechanism...I think.

Anyway, I went into an uncontrollable fit of laughter. In my head, I was swearing to god to please let her be okay. And, 'oh shit. Oh my god'. A classmate told me to shut the hell up and stop laughing. I sobered up and ran over to her to see if she was going to be okay. My classmates were pissed and there was a mix of staring at her and glaring at me. We all knew we were going to be in trouble. There was a trickle of blood dripping from the top of her skull, down her neck, and had begun to stain her clothes. Most kids didn't know what to do. They sat at their desks with their hands folded in their laps praying to god that everything would be okay. One kid ran out the classroom screaming, "Mr. H! Mr. H!, Mr. H!, where is Mr. H!?" One kid was crying. A group of kids had encircled the girl who was bleeding and were trying to comfort her. She was scared and crying (and mostly likely in shock). I tried to apologize to her, but she, and rightfully so, yelled at me to get the hell away from her. This was another one of those situations where I didn't mean it and it wasn't technically anyone's fault – it was one of those things.

Mr. H finally came back to the classroom and with a scowl on his face only said, "What the heck happened here?" A group of kids ran over to him and all tried to explain it at once. He calmed everyone down, pointed at one of my close friends, and said, "Only you. Tell me what happened". He explained it to Mr. H. The paper game, the kicking of the paper and then he pointed at me and said, "It was his shoe, Mr. H. He did it". Thanks friend for completely selling me out without even a millisecond of hesitation. It was my shoe. I walked up to Mr. H and explained that it was in fact my shoe and that "I was very sorry. I didn't mean it. I didn't know my shoe would come off that way". Was Leslie okay?"

Mr. H was a reasonable guy. He understood full well what happened and no one got into trouble that day. The girl with the hole in her head was taken to the emergency room where she received no more than five stitches; three deep and two superficial. I think we were lucky. It could have been a lot worse, you know, if the shard were larger, you know, had there been slightly more opportunity for greater gravity. She was back at school two days after the event. We never played the classroom paper game again.

I don't remember if the parents ever found out about the destruction caused by the paper game. I recall no form of punishment specifically related to this event so I can assume that Mr. H kept it under wraps.

Chapter 7

Shortly after the head-piercing event an evil, perhaps best defined as psychopathic, mindset took me over. I started to act criminally. I crafted devious plans and paid very careful attention to all of the details. I became extremely aware of my surroundings such as smells, noises, and patterns of the behavior of others. I acted destructively towards objects but not towards people. I can tell you some of what I did, but I don't believe I can recall why. Perhaps it was an attempt to seek out attention. Perhaps, I just wanted to test the boundaries of what I could get away with. And for a long time, I did get away with it.

I have described to you already that I was attending a private, Christian (Lutheran) grade school. Attached to the grade school was the church that the family was members of. *She* sang in the choir, therefore, I was forced to also sing in the choir. I didn't particularly enjoy the long hours of choir practice or the actual act of singing in front of the congregation. In fact, I think I recall intense emotions of disdain. I think I recall voicing, in whatever manner I could articulate at that age, that I didn't want to participate but *she* wanted me to do it. In order to avoid the "hurt" and the confrontation, I had no choice but to go along with it. My dad was quiet on this issue (Asshole).

One Sunday morning, we arrived extremely early to church. My dad was (still is) an Elder and he was busy attending to his Elder duties. *She* had attended the early service and had decided not to escort me to the later service. I was dropped off and I found myself wandering to the choir room where I was alone and was left to my own devices. Time passes slowly for an active, highly imaginative, young mind. I had nearly an hour to wait for any other soul to arrive.

I explored the room. There were lockers which housed the choir robes. I looked for something to steal like money, toys, books, pens, or pictures and found nothing that I valued. Only 5 minutes had passed. There was a piano in the room. I had been taking organ lessons so I sat on the bench and pounded out a tune or two using what I learned during my organ lessons. Without an audience, I was bored. Only 5 more minutes had passed. While still on the bench, I noticed hymnals and piano books resting comfortably on the music rack. The hymnals and the piano books contained all of the music, notes, and verses that the choir practiced with prior to each service. And...there was a black marker.

For no reason, other than perhaps to merely pass the time, I began to graffiti the hymnals and the piano books. Before I continue, I do want to say, that I am not proud of this act. At the time, I felt this action was justified. Anyway, I took the black, permanent marker and penned vulgar words throughout all of the pages. Let me manage your perception so that you know how evil this act really was.

I didn't just simply pen in vulgar words but enacted a detailed plan to ensure that I would not be caught. I write left handed. I intentionally switched my writing hand to my right hand so that if confronted, I could pen words in my true writing form and throw my confronters off of my path. In addition, with my non-writing hand, I intentionally made each word I documented in box-like letters. I scrawled them in a robotic font. That's not yet the worst of it. There was careful (evil) consideration for the placement of each dirty word. You see, I couldn't document these words on the cover of any book because it would be noticed immediately. I intentionally chose pages of each book that might cause the user to discover this act at random while they here haphazardly skimming through the pages. And then there what was I actually wrote; words and phrases such as:

God is an asshole. God is dead. Fuck you. Stupid cock sucking mother fuckers. Shitholes. Butt fuckers.

And so on and so forth. In total, I believe I had the time to graffiti and ultimately destroy nearly 15 hymnals and 3 piano books. As I later learned, these can be quite pricey. Although it's obvious, I should mention that those with the prospective discovery are bible abiding citizens of the church – and how could anyone entering their house of God commit such evil acts – the audacity!

The hour finally passed and I could hear footsteps walking towards the room. I ran to the choir practice benches and comfortably took my seat as though nothing happened. I slowed my breath. I adjusted my face and eyes to an innocent look. I casually and politely acknowledged the individual that entered the room.

Good morning Mr. H!

Mr. H, the third grade teacher, and also the music director / conductor for the school and church responded.

Good morning, Gavi! You're here early. Have you been here long?

No, Mr. H. I just got here. I am looking forward to the service today.

Me too, Gavi. Me too. Pastor H has a great message for all of us today; I'm sure of it.

I smiled. He smiled back. And soon the room was full of my classmates. We warmed up for the upcoming service and walked out in single file to the sanctuary. We sang our songs, reveled in the Word, and went on our merry ways without incident. My mind went to that dark place and I was gleaming with pride that I had not been caught.

Four days later Cheryl came home from choir practice. She was visibly flustered. She announced to my dad that choir practice did not occur this evening. Instead, Mr. H and the rest of the adult choir reviewed and discussed the graffiti to "God's sacred elements". She described in simple detail what had occurred. Then there was silence. The silence was a sign to my evil mind that the parents were telepathically contemplating whether or not their son was capable of such an act. They, in unison, turned their heads to glance in my direction. I was not confronted that night.

Two weeks went by and I was feeling very confident that I was not caught and would not be punished. It was a glorious and exhilarating feeling. I took it to the next level. Again, for some reason, I was left alone but this time within the grade school itself. I believe it was due to a track or sporting event I was participating in, like indoor soccer. Anyway, I had a black marker and I proceeded to graffiti the men's restroom. I used the same strategy as before with the non-writing hand, the block letters, and etc. I even wrote the same kind of vulgar descriptions on the restroom walls, above the urinals, and within the stall walls. It took me nearly 45 minutes. No one walked in. I discarded the marker, washed my hands, and rejoined the sporting event. Same innocent smile, eyes, and face as before.

That Monday, the principal broke the news to all grades, to all students, and to all teachers. He announced that there were two graffiti events within the past two weeks. He announced that the offending individual would be caught and punished accordingly. He announced that if the individual came forward now, and admitted their guilt, that they wouldn't be expelled and only suspended. If they didn't come forward now, and it was discovered who committed these "evil acts" that this individual would be expelled without hesitation.

My pulse quickened with anxiety. With that said, I felt that because of the way this was conveyed to the school that they really didn't have a suspect and therefore I really had nothing to worry about. Play it cool. In the moment of the announcement, I acted just like anyone else my age should act. I acted surprised, shocked, and astonished that someone could do such things. I looked to my left, I looked to my right, and my classmates were all doing the same thing as I was. They each looked left, and looked right. We all thought, 'Who could it be? Why would someone do something like this? Did you do it? I didn't do it. Who do you think did it?'.

The principal and the teachers came up with a plan to identify the culprit. They called a parent-teacher conference for all parents of all students for all grades. Of course the situation was explained to the parents. At the end of the conference, each set of parents was given an envelope with one 8.5"x11" piece of paper inside. On the piece of paper there were typed words. Each word was hand chosen by the school staff to represent the cumulative total of all of the letters used in the graffiti. Examples of words like, "mother, it, ship, Exodus, Flock". The parents were instructed to place this paper in front of their child, and next to each word, have their child print and write (in cursive) each word. Then, bring the paper back to their child's homeroom teacher for evaluation.

I remember my dad setting this piece of paper down on the table in front of me.

Gavi. You be honest with me right now! Are you responsible for the graffiti?

Calmly, coolly, and evenly I responded.

No dad. What did it say?

I knew by his facial gestures, body language, and voice tone that he suspected it was me. *She* was off in the background acting only as a witness. He grabbed me by the arm and asked me again. Except this time, he put his face as close to my face as possible without actually touching me. I responded the same way except this time, I made myself look like I was scared. I wasn't scared, but I put the face on anyway. At this early age I was figuring out that appearances and perception resembled something close to reality.

Ok Gavi. Here's what we're going to do. See these words? Next to each word, I want you to write the word both printed and in cursive. Understand?

Yes dad. I understand. Just right next to it?

Yes. Next to it. And I'm going to sit here and watch so don't try anything funny.

I thought, 'Funny? What could I possibly do in this situation other than what was asked of me'. I looked at the words and thought quickly and very carefully about what I had written and my actions in the choir rehearsal room and the men's restroom. I reconsidered my strategy of those two days with the block letters, switching hands etcetera and with very little hesitation yet an enormous amount of confidence began to pen the words in printed and cursive fashion. For a little extra flair, I exaggerated the cursive strokes more than usual. I thought, 'I got this. I'm so good'. When I was done, I looked up at my dad, smiled, and said, "all done, dad". He looked at me as though he were annoyed by the whole situation and walked out of the room. I can only imagine that he was contemplating what it would actually mean if I was found guilty of these actions. What would it mean to the Donato namesake to have his only son expelled from the church where he not only worshipped his God, but worse, in that he was looked at as a leader – an Elder. It certainly would be *the* talk of the town. I mean, what kind of parents would raise such a *devil*.

I presumed he turned in the paper as instructed. And to be quite honest, from my perspective, that's the end of that story. My strategy worked and I did in fact, get away with it. I was not confirmed as the individual responsible. In fact, no one was confirmed as the individual responsible. No one was suspended and no one was expelled. The school staff was unable to resolutely identify the individual. After, the restroom was repainted and the books were replaced. And wouldn't you know it, there were no other instances of graffiti at that school for as long as I attended.

One year later at age nine in the fourth grade I took on a different form of mischievousness. The fourth grade teacher was an absolute knockout, and for a nine year old, I had already begun to notice attractive ladies like her. I had a puppy-dog love kind of crush on Miss S perhaps taken too far for being nine. She was approximately 6'4", with blonde hair, blue eyes, and very slender. All of the boys liked her. Her lips were full and pouty and she always had bright red lipstick on. One day she was teaching the class about chemistry and brought up all of the great "experiments" we would be completing in the school year. In a little boy fantasy, I mumbled something under my breath.

I'd like to experiment with Miss S' breasts. I'd like to take them right in my hands and…

The little girl sitting in front of me heard what I said word for word and turned around and looked at me with a shocked face.

You can't say things like that.

What? I didn't say anything.

Yes you did! I'm telling! I'm telling! You talked about experimenting on Miss S's boobs!!

And then she told. She told the whole class. She literally verbalized what I said, word for word, as loud as she could for the whole class to hear. Miss S' face turned bright red and she promptly and unexpectedly exited the classroom. The boys in the class were laughing. The girls in the class were scowling at me but I could tell from their faces, they were also curious about "experiments with breasts". It was a bitter sweet moment, really. The principal arrived shortly after Miss S' exit, grabbed me by the arm and ushered me to his office. I don't remember what happened in his office. What I remember next is that Miss S escorted me back to the classroom. I was red in the face from embarrassment. She bent over at the waist and met me at my level. She had a v-shaped, low-cut top on, and when she bent at the waist to meet my eyes, I could see the beautiful top swells of her breasts and the bright red, lacy braw she was wearing. I felt a warm, tingling in my loins and my pulse quickened. She was staring directly into my eyes. I was staring down her shirt. I was *not* being a gentleman. She stood there in that position and patiently waited until I lifted my gaze. I looked into her eyes. My breaths were heavy. I thought we would kiss. Her eyes were huge and beautiful and I was in love.

Gavi, you owe me an apology. I want an apology right now.

She smiled and I noticed a dimple in her right cheek. Realizing the gravity of the situation, I put my head back on straight and I remembered: Always be a gentleman. Do the Donato namesake proud.

Yes ma'am. I am very sorry for what I said. It won't happen again.

Thank you.

She stood upright and then handed me a note.

Take this note home tonight and give it to your parents immediately. I expect a response from your parents by the end of the week. Friday. You understand, right Gavi?

Yes ma'am.

Deep within my subconscious I had been hoping that the trip to the principal's office plus the apology would have been sufficient. My heart and hopes sank when I was handed a note to deliver to my parents. When I got home that night, evil took me over. My parents had been planning for some time to take a vacation to Walt Disney Land and we were heading out on that Monday.

According to my plotting and scheming mind, it meant that I had to figure out a way to reconcile this issue and somehow still get to go on the vacation. I was excited about the vacation. To my recollection, I had never been on a vacation before and I had heard such great things about Disney Land; the rides, roller coasters, Captain EO (Michael Jackson was my favorite performer back then) and of course, Mickey & Minnie Mouse.

By this age the fear had been instilled in me. For the good kid I was (although you could debate that), for the great grades I received, for rarely getting into too much trouble (for not getting caught), I was not to be trusted and I was to be micromanaged to the Nth degree. Everything had to be controlled. There was also the fear of the parent's wrath, particularly *hers,* and the way *she* handled me. Nothing was ever good enough especially if things weren't completed in the manner *she* felt they should. (And let's remind ourselves Dear Reader, who the hell was *she*? Barely a high school graduate unable to hold a "real" job in the "real" world. An uneducated housewife, but I digress.) I was absolutely certain that if the parents gained knowledge of this event I would be punished in a manner that kept me from going on the vacation. I know that sounds a little strange and I do not mean to imply that I would be physically assaulted (although I will get to a few instances). I can only recall a few spankings in my life, actually, and most of those were from grandma. Anyway, the point is that I thought they would ground me and send me to *her* parent's house while they enjoyed a break from me. This, in my mind, was absolutely devastating. It would be more time that I didn't get to spend with my dad and I found this to be unacceptable so I came up with a plan.

When I got home that night, I opened the note and read it in excruciating amounts of detail. I read it over and over and made sure I understood all of the instructions and all of the nuances. I needed a solid plan if I was going to be able to go on this vacation.

Miss S explained the whole situation, word for word, and included a return note. The return note was supposed to be signed by my parents indicating that 1) they received it 2) they discussed the event with me and 3) that they also needed to issue an apology.

Numbers two and three were easy in my mind. I could lie and tell Miss S that in fact, my parents had discussed the event with me, that they were very disappointed in me, that they didn't raise me to act in this manner, and that it was not very Christian-like of me. (Because I had heard these words on many occasions leading up to this event.) I could then follow that up with, "they send their sincerest apologies". And finally, I could end the lie with, "and I too, Miss S, I am again, so very sorry". I imagined more deep staring in the beautiful eyes and longed for more top-breast sightings.

The problem with what Miss S wanted was the signatures by both of my parents. I thought very hard about how I could achieve this. I don't remember exactly how many options I schemed, but I do remember how I actually acted. I snuck into my parent's home office and stole two return address labels. Where the signature lines were was where I placed the return address labels. In my mind this was the perfect alternative. In addition to the previous and imaginary fibs, I made up a new one where I suggested that my parents were so busy, that they often times use address labels as their signature, and that because of the quick turn-around time, that being Friday, this was the best they could do.

The very next day I acted on all of this. I handed her the note, explained everything, and apologized once more. She received it all with a stoic face and simply said, "thank you, Gavi". I was in the clear. Like my other plans with the graffiti, this plan also worked!

I knew, deep within my subconscious that in reality, there was absolutely no way this plan would work. But for the time being, I seemed to be in the clear. I had day dreams about how fun it would be to scamper about Disney Land, going on roller coaster rides and the like; it was after all just right around the corner. I only had to make it through two more days. If applicable, I'd suffer the consequences later!

That night the phone rang. My mom answered the phone and I distinctly heard my mom announce who it was. My pulse quickened and I became anxious. I knew I was in for it. There was absolute silence from my mom. She was actively listening with an occasional, "Oh. Oh my. He did what?". When Miss S had finished telling the story to my mom, my mom calmly said, "Manlio, you're going to want to take this call. You're not going to believe what *your* son did".

Then it was my dad's turn. He listened to Miss S intently. Occasionally he muttered, an "Oh geez" and "Really?". When all was said and done, he apologized to Miss S profusely and informed her that, "Gavi will be disciplined accordingly. I can assure you". Again, our sincerest apologies to you Miss S; that is quite embarrassing".

Gavi! Sit your ass down.

'Oh shit' was my first thought. My dad was furious. But not about what you might think.

Gavi, do you have any idea what I'm mad about?

Yeah dad. You're mad because I wanted to experiment with Miss S' boobs.

He wanted to laugh but he maintained his composure.

No. No, that's not it at all, son. In fact, I am kind of relieved to hear that you're into girls. Just be careful. Anyway, what have I always said and what did your Grandma teach you? Always be a gentleman! Do you think you're being a gentleman by announcing out loud you want to manhandle your teacher's boobs? You forged our names. Where did you learn such behavior? It's so devious! What you did, took careful planning, and execution and you carried this out. It's malicious! Did it ever occur to you just to give

106

us the note that Miss S sent home with you? Just tell us and talk to us about what happened?

He paused.

No dad. It didn't occur to me to just tell you this and give you the note.

Why not, Gavi? Are we not approachable?

I didn't really understand back then what that might mean – *approachable.* I responded nonetheless.

I was worried that you wouldn't take me on the vacation; that I wouldn't get to go to Disney Land and that you would force me to stay with her parents. I did this so that I could delay my punishment and just deal with it later.

Oh, Gavi. Why would you have an idea like this in your head? You know you can talk to us about anything right?

I was dumbfounded and just stared into space. I actually didn't know I could talk to them about anything. Especially *her.* Anything I brought up to *her* was always perceived as some kind of mortal sin and that I most certainly was going to hell for acting like myself. I was always living in fear and walking around the place like I was stepping on uncracked eggs. I could only think of one thing to say.

She's always taking things away from me.

It was the most natural of thoughts for me. I didn't live up to the expectation, therefore, the consequence, as my deductive logic was telling me, was that, any and all privileges that I currently enjoyed, would be stripped one by one. No more outside play-time. No more television. No snacks. And of course, why would I be allowed to go on vacation? The word itself, in our household was held in the highest regard implying it was a privilege and therefore one of the first things to be stripped of. It seemed fitting that the punishment would have fit the crime.

My dad got it. He understood exactly what I said, but more importantly, what, if I had the vocabulary, I really meant to say.

Gavi. I'm going to talk this over with your mother. We'll let you know soon what your punishment will be.

He walked off. And just like the time I destroyed Teddy, they were alone in private conference deliberating on what my punishment should be. I was not privy to any of the discussion as the conferencing occurred behind closed doors.

The next day my dad announced what my punishment would be. He handed me a spiral notebook. Inside was scrawled one sentence. I would soon learn that this sentence was the template I would follow to write my own sentences.

Gavi. Tomorrow we leave for Florida to Disney Land. On our way, you will write the sentence that's listed there 10,000 times. Or, you'll write it until there's no more space on either side of the page of this spiral notebook, whichever comes first. Not only will you write 10,000 sentences, but you'll write them so that they are legible. I need to be able to read each word of each sentence. Do you understand?

Yes. I understand.

Hold on. One more thing. You will not be able to play at Disney Land until you've satisfied the terms of this punishment. Do you understand?

I think so. I have to write 10,000 sentences or fill up this notebook, whichever comes first, and I have to do this before I can have any fun on vacation.

You're a smart boy, Gavi. That's exactly right. Do you have any questions?

No dad.

I'm disappointed in what you did Gavi. You have shamed your father's name. You completely embarrassed one of your elders. It is not easy to stand up in front of all of you sniveling, punk kids and try to teach them how to get through life. You should have more respect for Miss S! Do you think she wants to hear, from a little boy, how that little boy wants to fondle her privates? Think about it, Gavi. When we get back, I want you to show Miss S what we had you do, and I want you to sincerely apologize on behalf of your parents and on behalf of yourself. You can redeem your honor by completing this exercise. ot it?

Yes dad. I'm really sorry.

One more thing. Don't you ever forge our name again. I won't be so forgiving if there's a next time. I will bring out the belt.

There was nothing more that needed to be said. The *belt*, as far as my little-boy brain was concerned, was an instrument of evil, torture, and death. From my little-boy perspective, it was as wide as it was long, and the long, leather strap was studded lengthwise with holes covered by metal. Those metal covered holes caused my rear-end significant stinging when it struck my bare bottom.

We began our long drive from mid-Michigan to Florida and I began my quest to write 10,000 sentences or to run out of spiral notebook pages, whichever came first. The template sentence that my dad had crafted read like this:

I will not forge my parent's name on any document ever, in my lifetime. I will think about my actions before I act. I will not embarrass my teachers, my parents, my grandparents, or myself. I will do the Donato namesake proud.

That certainly is a lot to write, in one sentence. I have nothing negative to say about this. And even to this day, I do feel that the punishment fit the crime. It was one of the few times that I can remember, where something I did wrong, was handled calmly, collectively, and without an overabundance of drama or emotions.

I completed the exercise by the time we arrived to Florida by developing a writing system. I developed my own sentence template by creating rows and columns in the spiral notebook paper. Each column corresponded to a particular word. In this way, I could write the same word down the entire column, and then repeat for the next word. It looked something like this:

I will not forge my parent's name on   any document

I will not forge my parent's name on   any document

And so on…The system was ingenious and I completed page after page in record time. My column lines were very faint, and the notebook was never scrutinized to a level where my system was questioned. In addition, I had my Sony Walkman to keep me motivated, listening to Michael Jackson, Paul Abdul, Bon Jovi, Guns 'N' Roses, and the Beastie Boys. (*Gavi! Turn your music down; you'll go deaf!*)The time, the pages, and the states fluttered by and in practically no time, I was enjoying the hot, humid weather of Disney Land, Florida.

Every so often, *she* would look at me in the back seat and yell at me about how loud my music was. If *she* could hear it in the front seat, then it was clearly too loud, and "you'll go deaf, don't ya know?". I complained back, that I could barely hear my own music in my ears and that she could only hear it because "she strained herself to listen". I remember my dad laughing at this and her complaining to him, "Manlio, you make your son listen to me". "Leave him alone, Cheryl" was his response. And so, I was left alone. And I can still hear to this day, don't ya know?

Chapter 8

In the fifth grade I tried and succeeded in becoming more active in sports. In the fifth grade, I was about 4'6". Mr. B was the fifth grade teacher. He was a California transplant and had a Southern California disposition. He was tall and lean standing at approximately 6'6". He towered over most of us, and when I stood in front of him to speak, I had to stare straight up into the sky to meet his eyes. Mr. B was the coolest grade school teacher out of them all. The first lesson I learned from Mr. B was that it was okay to lose sometimes.

Every once in a while, Mr. B would give the class a break from academics and take us into the gym for exercise. One of the class' favorite gym-games was floor hockey. I believe Mr. B liked to conduct his own, personal social experiments. For example, one day, Mr. B decided to split the class into two teams. One team of boys and the other of girls. Except that he, Mr. B, to "even the odds" was going to play on the girl's team. No problem.

The game started and the boys took a commanding lead. By the end of the second period the boys were up 3 – 0. With one period to go, the boys knew they "had it in the bag". Then, Mr. B took over. By the middle of the third quarter Mr. B scored three goals single handedly. The boys were worried. As time expired,

Mr. B fired a shot and scored the winning goal. The proverbial crowd went wild and the girls all screamed with delight at *their* win. As was our custom, we lined up in single file to walk back to the classroom.

I was pissed. I was in disbelief that we (the boys) lost. And while I was standing in line, hidden by all of the other children in line, I verbally pronounced my displeasure. In a hurt tone, and on the verge of crying I voiced my anger.

They only won because of you, Mr. B! If you hadn't been on the team, they would've lost. It's not fair.

The thunder cracked.

Who said that!!?

Mr. B hurried to a location in the gym where we could all see him. With his hands on his hips he said:

I want to know who said that right now!

The line of children parted like the Red Sea and I was left standing alone. I could feel the heat of everyone's gaze. At last, understanding that there was no way to displace the blame, I raised my hand.

I said it. And I meant it!

Get over here right now, Gavi!

I walked over to him. Internally, I was panicked. The whole class was watching and I had no idea what was going to happen. When I was standing in front of him, he bent down at the waist to my level and said:

Do you want to say that to my face?

Sure. The girls won the game only because you were on their team. It's not fair!

Life's not fair, Gavi.

To that logic I was left with no other choice but to throw a temper tantrum. I know what you're thinking. In the fifth grade we are too old to throw public temper tantrums and I agree with you, Dear Reader. However, it is, nevertheless, what I did. In my ridiculous dress shoes and dress pants, I proceeded to stomp on the floor with my dominant right foot. I was yelling, "It's not fair" over and over again and even had the nerve to point my finger in Mr. B's face and scream unintelligibly. Had it been intelligible I think it would have said something sophomoric like, "it's because of you".

Once the screaming started, Mr. B's disposition changed from cool-eyed understanding to surprised bewilderment. Obviously I

116

needed a life lesson and Mr. B was a man of action to promptly provide one. He scooped me off the ground and swung me around in the air while making airplane noises. Ridiculous right? The whole class was pointing and laughing at me. My face was red, I was thoroughly embarrassed, and I started crying. I was not just crying. It was the type of crying where the face is scrunched, the tears are forming streams on the cheek bones, and snot bubbles were forming at the nostrils. It was the kind of cry where you cannot quite get enough oxygen down the throat and so you uncontrollably sob, like a hiccup. I was absolutely humiliated.

Are you done yet, Gavi? Why are you crying?

I don't. I. I don't know.

It's all going to be okay, Gavi. You're not going to win every time, Gavi. Sometimes Life is not going to be fair and you're going to have to learn how to manage through it. It's unacceptable for a man to behave the way you're behaving. You might think this is the end of your world. This is where it starts. This is where you get the chance to start making decisions for yourself. Do you want to be the kind of man where people are pointing and laughing at you? Or do you want to be the kind of man that people admire and respect? You have the choice. It's up to you. Take a few moments to collect yourself.

He then patted me on the behind and told me to get back in line. He then announced to the class that –

There will be times in [our] lives where we just need to let it all out. This was one of Gavi's times. It takes courage to stand up for what you believe is right, and Gavi displayed that courage today. I admire him for what he did, just not how he did it. There is a correct way to convey your message. The real lesson learned today is that none of us know what is going on in the lives of those that are right in front of us so don't be so quick to pass judgment. Ok. Good game everyone. Rematch, with the same teams at the end of the week.

What a great guy. We had that rematch and lost that one too. But I acted gracefully remembering Mr. B's words. Everyone looked up to Mr. B with respect and seemed to understand. None of my classmates ever brought up my humiliation directly to me and instead it was all business as usual. I often wondered, in my later years anyway, if Mr. B knew what was going on at home leading up to this event – sometimes *we just need to let it out*. Regardless, this was something that Mr. B kept between the class because I was never approached by my parents about it.

Unfortunately, I did get in trouble for some other, more personal issues.

In grade 5, I began to understand differences in people. I could understand differences in skin color and I also started to acknowledge differences in gender and the laws of attraction. Obviously I knew I was attracted to girls and, ahem, wanted to experiment. And girls were attracted to me. I didn't know how to handle certain situations, because as *she* had always iterated, "[I] had better keep it in my pants until [I] was married or [I] would be condemned to the fires of hell".

I remember very distinctly, when I learned of my personal power of attraction. This very cute girl, Mindy, sat down across from me one day, looked me dead in my eyes, fluttered her eyes at me and said, "I am so lost in your eyes". She then leaned across the desk and planted a wet kiss on my lips. My face went red. I was dumbfounded and said nothing except, "thank you". It must have taken her some nerve to walk across the room, sit down in front of me, say what she said, lean, kiss, and then walk away. It certainly is a personal, vivid memory. I never followed up with Mindy so it was a first and last event as I like to say.

Shortly after the first and last kiss from Mindy, I realized there was a boy in the class who was not like the rest of the boys. He did not yet like girls. What could possibly be wrong with him? I mean girls smelled nice, talked nice, looked nice, and were great to be around. Someone in the class pointed out to me that the boy was gay. I didn't understand. I didn't know this term. I looked it up in the dictionary. The dictionary we had at the school at the time simply defined the term in the sense of being happy. This further confused me. What does being happy have to do with his like or dislike of girls? That same someone then defined for me what it meant to be gay: Boys having sex with other boys. I, of course, was shocked. We were being taught that only men and women were "to be together" and that to be *that way* was an unforgivable sin worthy of hell and eternal damnation.

Obviously because of my upbringing, I felt obligated to change this boy's mind. His name was Andy and I believe what I did to him most likely had an impact on his outlook on life for the rest of his life. I'm not proud of this. As a Southern California resident, DoYoung and I are fully aware of and accepting of people, in general, regardless of sexual orientation. In fact, we have many gay friends. It's uncomfortable only at times where they want to have a dialogue about bedroom activities, but otherwise it's like having conversations with anybody. And why wouldn't it be? People are people, people!

Anyway, I sought Andy out. Sort of. The class was outside at recess. We were all playing our "battle games" on the playground equipment. I instigated an event with Andy. I insisted that I go down the slide first. Andy was okay with that. Then, each time, over several instances I kept insisting I go down the slide first. I ran as fast as I could to get to the slide, and then intentionally waited for Andy to arrive just so that I could insist that he wait while I go down the slide. He grew visibly frustrated. When I turned my back to go down the slide, he jumped on my back. The classmates were watching this whole event unfold and were waiting for that one moment where group think could take over. When he jumped on my back, group think, in fact, did take over and not more than a few moments passed where the class was yelling, "Fight! Fight!" in unison.

The entire class formed a circle around us. Andy was still on my back and actually had an arm around my head and neck in a choke hold although I wasn't actually being choked. The class was encouraging me to kick Andy's ass. "Kill that faggot. Beat his ass" were some of the phrases tossed around. I saw red and did what I set out to do in the first place – to convince him, through violence (apparently) that 1) it was wrong to like other boys and 2) that he needed to like girls immediately or he was going to hell.

(Oh man. When I write these words I feel completely ashamed. At the same time, this is how my asshole parents, in the ridiculous Christian curriculum, raised me to feel and think. Children do not make this stuff up on their own in the fifth grade! Paradoxically, we're also taught that if we don't keep it in our pants, we're going to hell for that too! It's a wonder we don't all turn out to be asexual! And, no wonder we're all so confused and conflicted when we finally start allowing ourselves to experience the physical aspects of adulthood).

I grabbed Andy's arm from around my neck and pealed it away. Still having a hold on his arm, I somersaulted him to the ground. I jumped on top of him, straddled him, and beat him up by punching him in his stomach and face (just like in the destruction of Teddy). It was over in a few seconds, seconds I wish I could take back.

Someone, much stronger than a fifth grade student, ripped me off of Andy. Of course it was Mr. B. He grabbed both of us, each of us, by one arm and dragged us to the principal's office.

We sat together outside of the principal's office anxiously waiting for our punishments. Andy's face was already starting to bruise on both cheeks. His upper lip was swollen and one of his nostrils was filled with blood. He was holding his stomach. He wouldn't look at me. He had not landed one of his punches and other than the holes in the knees of my pants, you would not know that I had been in a fight. At the time, I was proud. All of my classmates marveled in my victory as I was, and would continue to be, the shortest of all the male, children.

The principal, in typical fashion wanted to get to the bottom of this. He started and ended with me.

Gavi! What is this about?

Andy is gay. I wanted him to not be gay anymore.

The principal did not expect this. He had expected something more predictable. As in, Andy wouldn't give me the ball. Or Andy, called me a name. You get the point. He handed Andy some Kleenex to dry his eyes and his nose. He scrawled a note, handed it to me, told me I was in big trouble, and to give this note to my parents. Remembering my former lessons regarding Miss S, I promptly gave the note to my parents when they picked me up and told them truth when they questioned me. *She* took the lead on this one and all that was said was this:

Gavi. You don't punch people in the face. People can get really hurt by getting punched in the face. You could kill someone by punching them in the face. Then we would get sued and lose all of our money. You don't want that do you? Do you? Don't punch people in the face. You're grounded.

Okay. From that I took away that it was okay to fight as long as I didn't punch them in the face. I guess it was also okay to try and convince someone they were not gay. And of course, a recurring theme, don't do anything that would impact the finances. Great. Got it. I won't punch people in the face. Good parenting, asshole. Thank you for clearly communicating the most critical aspects of the situation so that I would learn from my mistakes. It's okay, I knew what my mistakes were and I did learn from them without the parental guidance.

Andy was absent from school for a few days. I left walloping bruises on his face and in order to literally save face, Andy, his parents, Mr. B, and the principal felt it would be best if Andy took a week off of school. I was suspended for a few days but neither of those things helped me learn the lesson. When Andy came back to school he had a different disposition. Before the fight he was outgoing. After, he was introverted. He kept to himself, kept quiet, and never really looked any of us in the eyes again. Often, we would catch Andy talking to himself and answering his own questions. He grew pale and disengaged. Because I notice these details, I tried approaching him and in all honesty, with the intent to befriend him. I did feel bad for what I had done so I also wanted to apologize. He cowered backwards and had wide eyes when he saw me walking towards him and I decided the timing was wrong. I never had another opportunity. Not more than a week later, Andy transferred to a different school and I never saw him again. I don't know what became of him or if he recovered. I hope he did. It was after all, a serious misunderstanding and we both were just young, punk kids. (and Andy if you're reading this and you'd like to connect, send me a message to the email address found at the back of this book).

Around this same time, I was playing on the monkey bars with a close, black friend of mine named Israel. For no reason at all, I called him a "dirty nigger". I don't know what came over me. I immediately and profusely apologized on the spot. He was such a close friend of mine, that he laughed it off although later in life, we grew distant, in my mind, because I think he thought I was a racist bastard. Obviously I'm not racist having married a Korean woman. And after having been in the military, I only really see that which matters to me the most: Demeanor & Intellect.

Anyway, Israel and his father, Felix were invited over to our house for dinner. And looking back on this memory, I can recall where I learned racism – from *her*. *She* had planted seeds of racism in my mind about how white people were far superior to the colored folks which is what *she* learned from *her* parents. This is actually confusing since they grew up in the time of the Nazis and The Holocaust. Anyway, maybe Israel and I grew apart because he realized my family was a bunch of racist bastards. I know DoYoung can attest to the racist mentality of my stepmother's (*her*) side of the family, so for now, Dear Reader, this story is about Israel and Felix is simple foreshadowing.

In the sixth grade, I got into another fight but slightly different. Another Andy wanted to establish dominance and decided he wanted to test his strength against mine. There were plenty of things I did as a kid which directly resulted in me being much stronger than I appeared for my 4'6" frame. Anyway, this Andy walked up to me calmly, faced me, put his hands on my shoulders, and without warning started to push me backwards as hard as he could.

Directly behind me were the classroom closets. The closet doors of this classroom were made of solid wood, were nearly four inches thick, and rested on a swivel track. The swivel track allowed the doors to fold in on itself so that both sides of that particular section of the closet could be accessed simultaneously.

Andy was about to shove me into these deathtrap doors, when instead, I gained my composure, and in my Sunday best attire, started to push back. Being shorter, had its advantage. My low center of gravity plus my self-proclaimed strength were going to establish me as the Alpha in this scuffle.

In mid-shove, I spun Andy around and with all of my might slammed him into the closet doors. The classroom went silent. Everyone watched, but in this case, no one said anything. I think everyone was waiting to see what would happen. I mean if you stop and think about the history for a second there are several events to consider where those as young as us have probably learned to just let it play out.

The shove into the closet doors was hard and loud. Andy made a thudding noise but the door itself made a rusty hinge, grinding type sound. I just happened to shove Andy into the door hard enough where the closet door became unhinged from the track. I noticed this immediately as I was also noticing the door beginning its low descent on a path to crush Andy.

It's true. The door was going to fall on Andy, and the weight of it would most likely kill him. I knew it. The class knew it. And thank goodness that's not what happened. Seeing the door starting to fall on Andy, I put myself in harm's way and with all of my strength pushed the door as hard as I could so that it would fall in the opposite direction. And that's exactly what happened. It fell in the opposite direction into all of the children's belongings instead of into the child or the children still sitting in their desks next to the doors. As it was falling, Andy and I had enough wherewithal to get out of the immediate vicinity. The door continued its fall into the belongings, scraping over all of the closet cubbies, before finally grinding to a halt on the tiled floor. It was loud. It was slow. Andy and I both knew that we were going to be in trouble for this. No one went to get a teacher this time.

Miss. H, the sixth grade teacher, was suddenly standing next to us. She lined up everyone in a row next to the closet doors and started to interrogate us. I knew that she knew it was probably my fault. And so, she started with me.

Gavi. I want you to tell me what happened here.

I was quick on my feet, don't ya know!

Yes, Miss H. Andy and I were just rough housing a little. We fell into the closet door and the closet door started to fall on us. Together, we were able to avoid the door from falling on us and we also pushed it away from Sarah, Joey, LeeAnn, and Markel.

How great is that. Miss H started to ask the other children what happened. All of them went along with my story. Andy even repeated it word for word. It was a huge win anyway you look at it. I mean, except for the obvious lie. I was learning very early on that if you don't get caught, you can't get into trouble.

And, thanks to how I was being parented, when everything I did was considered to be *wrong*, worthy of eternal damnation, I learned now to never get caught for anything.

Chapter 9

Around the sixth grade, I had hit puberty and life all together was changing. I was becoming aware. I was becoming aware of the changes in my body, aware of changes in the way I was thinking about any one thing at any one moment, and I was becoming aware of my own emotional disposition and reactions to stimuli. Particularly parental stimuli. And for whatever reason, my parents decided to send me to my grandparents for each summer between the sixth, seventh, and eighth grades.

I think, during the school year of the fifth grade, my dad started to notice an emotional change in me. What I haven't eluded to yet is how, during those grade school years my biological mother fit into this story. Here's how it would usually play out. My dad would receive a call from her. During that call, together they would arrange the *how* and *when* she might be able to take custody of me for a day, or for a night, or maybe even longer, schedule dependent. My father would then tell me that my *mother* would come to pick me up at such and such day on such and such time. Early on, I would get excited about the opportunity to visit with her, with her mom, and with her stepdad. I was too young then, to think that it was strange she was living with her parents.

Being excited about the visit, on the allotted day I would run back to my room, pack my own bag, and then near the allotted pick up time, patiently wait on the front porch for the biological mom to arrive. I believe I can recall over 100 times, spread out through a decade of my life, where I packed that bag and patiently waited only for the biological mother to never arrive. Believe me. This has an effect on a young mind that translates into a certain mindset within an older mind. The effect is quite definitively described as Abandoned child syndrome.

Imagine if you will, being somewhere between 5 and 15 years old, waiting, sometimes for hours, on a front porch, for your mom to come get you. That 6 or 7 year old, just sits there, with the elbows on the knees, and the hands on the face, and patiently waits by staring off into the horizon. Is that her car? No, that's just the neighbor. Is that her? No, that's just some stranger. And then, the day turns into night, and that 8 year old is still sitting there. He's hoping beyond reason that this time will be different. This time, she'll really show and pick me up and we'll listen to Michael Jackson together.

In my early twenties, many of my girlfriends had to deal with this issue with me. The issue and the fear of being abandoned. That's what that behavior does to the young mind. I didn't know how to articulate it in my early twenties but that's what it came down to. And only through dating women who were older than me could I ever really diagnose that that's what the problem was. Think about it. Rightly so, I was shipped up north in my formative years by my dad to be protected from the mom. Only later to be left on a porch step in the following years. And then constantly being told I would go to hell for basically breathing oxygen by *her*. I was messed up to start my twenties.

One time, when I was five years old, and shortly after my return to live with my dad and my new "mother" (*her)* the biological mother actually showed up to pick me up for a visit. My dad walked me down to the car, let me get in, and stood on the driver's side with his arms folded across his chest. My dad and my biological mom exchanged a few words.

I'm glad to see his bag is packed, Manlio. Did *she* pack it for him?

No. I think Gavi packed it himself this time.

Oh, really? What? Your retard of a wife couldn't figure it out?

She laughed and cast *that* look towards my dad. That one that says, "I'm fucking crazy, so watch what you say next you god-damned son-of-a-bitch". My dad responded accordingly.

Isn't your guardian supposed to be with you when you're driving the car? The guardian better god damned be at the house when you get Gavi there. Gavi, you call me when you get to the house. I want to talk to you.

I nodded 'yes' in confirmation. It was all very tense. I noticed that my dad's eyes were watering.

Take care Gavi. I love you.

I love you too, Dad.

I believe her mindset for that trip and for my visit was one of spite or perhaps revenge. In the same way my dad had kidnapped me from her, I believe she set out to do something as equally horrendous. Instead of arriving to the Guardians' house, we instead went to her grandmother's house. Now, her grandmother was just as much of a nut as she was. Immediately when we arrived, the grandmother handed me a loaded .38 revolver and told me to go outside and play. She told me, "it's a cap gun, Gavi. Have fun!".

As it turns out, she came to have the .38 revolver from her long dead husband who was able to keep the weapon after his retirement from the Detroit Police Department.

Anyway, I remember thinking that this is going to be so cool. I have a cap gun. I'm going to play Cops and Robbers. Or

Cowboys and Indians. So, in the middle of suburbia Detroit, I took that loaded .38 and began to shoot things. Now here's the tricky part. There was some time between receiving the handgun and actually going outside to play with it. Growing up mostly at my parents' house, and having friends in the neighborhood who were my age, I knew what a cap gun was. I knew the smell of the caps, the strings they came in to reload, and I also knew the weight. Even as a young, punk adolescent I was already paying attention to the details. I looked at my mom and asked a question.

Can I have the strips to reload?

No Gavi. It's already loaded. Listen to your great grandmother. Now go outside and play.

But. I'll go through the strips fast. Can I have more? I promise I'll be good.

What did I just say Gavi?! Get the hell outside and play.

Daddy told me I needed to call home as soon as I got here.

Your Father is not here is he, Gavi?

I decided this was a futile discussion. Everyone in the house was eyeing me and as I looked around the room they all had stupid smirks on their face with insane twinkling in the eyes. I remember there being at least three other people in the room but I have no idea who they were.

I knew I didn't have a cap gun in my hand. I knew it was a real gun. It was heavy and the metal was cold. Cap guns are plastic and light. What I didn't know was that it would NOT be okay to go outside and play with it. I took the gun outside as I was instructed and I started "playing". At this point, I had not ever fired a real gun before. I held it up and aimed it and then held it back down. To be honest, I think I was scared.

I saw my mom pull back the blinds on the window and all five individuals, whoever the other three were, were watching me with anticipatory excitement. My thirty-seven year old mind wishes I could travel back in time and pretend to raise that handgun up to aim at that window they were staring out of and pretend fire it. You know, fake some recoil after it pretend goes off. Can you imagine their shocked faces and the thought: "Oh shit! Well, this idea has obviously backfired". I'm laughing as I type that. Anyway, what really happened was not as good as the story I have been telling you so far. I knew I had a real gun. I treated it as such – cautiously.

I looked around and mostly what I had in front of me were houses, mailboxes, and cars. It was, afterall, suburbia Detroit in one of the local, residential neighborhoods. I thought about what to shoot and how to shoot it. As far as I could tell, there were no people around and there were no other kids. In the backyard, I aimed it at a pine tree and pulled the trigger. There was a loud sound, the usual recoil, and pine tree splinters filled the air. It appeared my aim was straight and true. That's a good thing considering if I had not hit the tree I would have hit the back of someone's house. I aimed it at a large rock in the ground, fired, watched the rock spark as the bullet hit it and I even laughed a little. In this same manner, I aimed it four more times, at immobile and lifeless objects that were mostly in the ground, pulled the trigger, watched the effect, chuckled, and just like that, the gun was out of bullets. Post script: I did all of this left handed.

Much to the disappointment of my mother, her grandmother, and whoever else was there that day, I didn't shoot any cars, houses, mailboxes, people, or myself. I'm sure I was lucky that some of the shots that I fired didn't ricochet and cause inadvertent damage or death. At least to my knowledge, nothing like that happened. Miraculously, I didn't injure myself either.

When I got home from that trip, in an excited manner, I told my dad all about it. When I was finished telling him the story, he raised an eyebrow and told me a story of his own.

Gavi.

Most of his stories started out this way. He wanted to get my attention so there would be the pronunciation of my name followed by a long pause for dramatic effect. When he felt he had my attention, then the story would begin.

When you were just a toddler, I don't know, not more than 3 years old, and just prior to me sending you up north to hang out with your grandparents I had to deal with that gun once before. I hated allowing you to visit your mother, her mother, and her mother's mother. That whole family is crazy. Wackadoodles. I'm being serious, Gavi. They are *crazy!* If I haven't mentioned it to you before, let me mention it now. Your mom has schizophrenia; it's a mental disorder. Anyway, I was letting that side of the family watch you for whatever reason, it escapes me now. It was time to pick you up. I drove over there and you were in your grandmother's arms. She was holding you. She had *that look* in her eye. I've seen it many times before and it scares the shit out of me. You just never know what's going to happen when she has *that look*. She was holding you.

I remember my dad's face having a real look of concern as he was trying to tell me this story. This story was not as fluid as his other stories. He was repeating himself. And now I also had to know everything there was to know about this thing my dad called *skitso-friendy-uh,* some kind of mental disorder.

You were oblivious. You were holding her back. In fact, you looked quite content to be held.

He laughed.

Anyway, your grandmother watched me walk towards the porch. I was about a few feet away from the porch when she said, "that's far enough; stop right there". I was shocked to hear such words so I stopped. "Your son won't take this pack of gum from me, and he won't eat any of the pieces. I keep telling him, that in order for his bones to grow strong and to be healthy, that he needs to eat this gum. He keeps telling me that you don't allow him to have gum. I want him to have this gum!" I replied, "We don't like him to have gum yet. It's bad for his teeth". She didn't like that response, Gavi, and she pulled out that .38 and stuck it to your head. I don't think you understood what was going on, but I can tell you I almost pissed my pants. She cocked the hammer back. I held up my hands in front of me and said, "Wait! Please, wait!". She waited. I said, "I'll take the pack of gum and I'll make sure he eats a piece". I guess that wasn't good enough because she took the gun off of you and pointed it directly at me. I stood dumbfounded for what felt like five minutes. When I finally regained my

137

bearings, I made a decision right there on the spot. I decided, that just like you can't argue with stupid, you also can't discuss with crazy. I made my feet move forward and began walking towards you and the porch. The gun was still pointed at me. I wrestled you from your grandmother's arms, turned my back, and began to walk steadily, progressively to the car. I never looked back. My heart was thudding in my chest and I swear I could hear the blood rushing in my ears. I got in the car, I didn't buckle you in or anything, and drove off as fast as I could. When the adrenaline wore off, I noticed that I was soaked in nervous sweat. Anyway Gavi, there wasn't anything else I could think of to do that day. I was happy that I got you home safely and that neither of us were shot. Shortly after, that old, crazy lady stroked out and died, God damn her soul to hell, thank you very much.

Rightly so, this retelling of the story stressed him out. He got up, poured himself a glass of wine, walked to the other room, turned on the television, and sat there sipping his wine pretending to watch whatever was on. I, not really knowing what I should do, went to my room to play. My memory of the event that my dad described centers on the only minor detail of the whole story – the pack of gum. I can remember it was a mint green package of Wrigley's Doublemint chewing gum.

So, Dear Reader, let's revisit the whole Biological Mother issue for a second. She was diagnosed to be mentally incapable, schizophrenic, and manic depressive. She was court ordered to live with a "Guardian". She had visiting rights of me whenever she was psychologically capable, She tried to kill me, she tried to rape me, and then she tried to turn me into a criminal. Do I have any good memories of this woman? Yes, I do, and I intend to represent more than just the dark side of the story.

Chapter 10

I can recall exactly two fond memories of the biological mother. And only those two so pay attention.

My Dad allowed me to visit with her and her parents for one of my birthdays but I can't recall which year. To my actual surprise, they threw me a surprise birthday party. I'll just cut to the bottom line on this memory. It was a fond memory because everyone who attended, which was hardly anyone I actually knew, brought me a card with a wad of money inside. It was actually the first time I remember interacting with people who weren't white as there were many interracial marriages within that side of the family.

When the party was over, I counted the cash and it was in excess of $500. I couldn't tell you what happened to that money once I got home. My suspicion is that the parents used this money to buy an educational "device". I can't recall the name so I texted my dad, and he also couldn't recall the name. Anyway, as he puts it in the text, they got me this contraption "so you wouldn't become a dumb shit. Must have worked". My reply, "Right. I was in first or second grade getting straight A's, so that makes total sense". (Asshole!)

Later, I called my dad about this device which he was calling, the "Spin-Teacher". This is what he told me.

Gavi, here's the story on the spin-teacher. Grandma, your step-mother's mother, got it for your mom because your mom needed some remedial help. She had difficulty in school because her ears were plugged up until she had an operation to open them up, so she could hear better. So when you were little, you used it mostly for math instruction. Now it resides with one of your white-trash cousins and her little bastard children. And now you know the rest of the story (Thanks, Paul Harvey).

Nice Dad. My first thought was this story seemed eerily similar to the multiple-bones-in-the-shoulder story. Sure…she needed her ears opened up, just like she can't wear sleeveless shirts

140

or dresses due to multiple bones. Anyway, my second thought was that I needed to verify the information. I'm making quite the substantial claim accusing my parents of using my gift money to buy me some contraption that I didn't even need.

Using my Dad's information, I surmised that if what he was saying was true, this device would have been associated to the 1960s. Using a search criteria in Google Images including terms like "1960s", "teacher" and "spin", and after scrolling through all of the images, I finally found it.

It's called the Cyclo-Teacher. I looked into this device as much as I cared to, which lasted all of about five minutes. The bottom line is that this contraption is in fact from the 1960s, so my Dad is right. I'll lead with that and let you know I don't mind if I have a few memories jumbled. I am after all, The Revisionist. I'm sure I'll be able to address where my $500 went at some point. Another search revealed that you can buy this top-tech from the 1960s for about $5.00 on auction sites. The *Schenectady Gazette*, from Schenectady, NY, November 14th, 1964, had this to say about the Cyclo-Teacher:

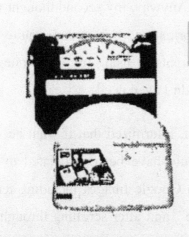

CYCLO-TEACHER®
LEARNING AID

An easy to use teaching machine scientifically developed to extend a child's interest. Creates confidence, aids retention, and helps students to approach school work with eagerness. Covers 233 subjects.

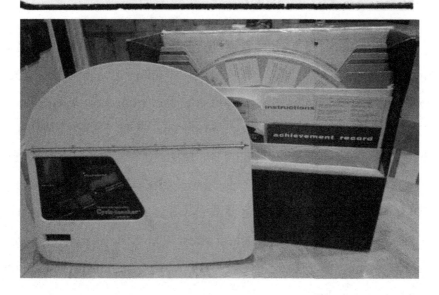

Golly. I know it helped my confidence and I certainly became more eager to get even straighter A's in school. I included a clearer Google Image of the device so that you'd have an idea in your mind. Honestly, it's one of those contraptions that you have to see to believe it. There would be no amount of words I could put to paper that would give you a clear vision of this thing. I showed DoYoung a picture of the Cyclo Teacher. She said, "Oh my God! That looks like a torture device!".

Anyway, I've digressed but also where did that $500 go (poof, gone). The second, and final pleasant memory of my biological mother involves my favorite musician of the time, Mr. Michael Jackson. My mom and I would spend hours, making mixed cassette tapes of whatever albums were available at the time but they were mostly Michael Jackson recordings from the radio. We'd sit on the living room floor, next to the stereo, she'd smoke cigarettes, I'd inhale second hand smoke and I'd wait for the right moment to hit record as the song came on the radio.

I was only interested in Michael Jackson at the time, but I do also recall recording the likes of Gloria Estefan and George Michael. I would take the cassettes home only to have them thrown out by *her* because "we don't listen to that kind of music in this house". That's correct ladies and gentlemen, in the Donato household, we listened to classical (nothing wrong with that), whatever *she* was playing and singing in falsetto on the household organ, usually Elvis fucking Presley, and 93.1 the Lite FM. Sometimes my Dad would get rebellious and crank up some Led Zeppelin. Sometimes, but hardly never.

Chapter 11

The rest of the memories are shit and involve abandonment, heartache, injury, and pain. I think, Dear Reader, if you can stomach it any further, I can recall two more memories to emphasize the point, and then that's it. It will be time to move on.

As I've mentioned, my biological mom and her guardians, my grandparents, lived together in a small house in inner city Detroit. Between the three of them they had two dogs. The two dogs couldn't be more different from each other. One dog was a young, dappled, short-haired energetic and yippity daschund. The other dog was old, plain black, long haired, lazy and a quiet bouvier. The bouvier's name was Bear, which was absolutely appropriate. Go ahead, take a moment to Google Image "bouvier". The daschund's name is lost to me by now and for purposes of this story it isn't worth reaching out to anyone just for the name of the dog. We'll call him Yippity.

One of my favorite games to play, while at my biological mother's house, was chase the dogs. I would chase them both at the same time. I'd chase them through a hallway into an adjoining living room, through the living room into an adjoining dining room, through the dining room, into the kitchen where the cycle would start over. The dogs loved it. I loved it. It was fun for everyone except the grumpy step-grandpa who after running a convenience store all day in a troubled and gang laden inner city Detroit, just wanted to come home, drag on a cigar, sip on a scotch, and melt into the couch while watching Wheel of Fortune and Jeopardy. Side note: He'd be even grumpier when we were making mixed tapes. He'd say, "I have to listen to that God-damned bee bop music all damn day in the store. Turn it off. I'm getting an ulcer and will have to eat green tomatoes". I had lots of questions about this, but none were answered. We just did what he said.

So, I'm chasing the dogs and it's starting to get late at night. Yippity has his tongue hanging out, his ears are flopping forwards and backwards with each little hot-dog step as he's scooting from room to room. His eyes are wild with delight. Bear, who doesn't have as much energy, participates in a few cycles, slops some water into his mouth, and lays down to watch us and eventually just falls asleep. Yippity and I have an endless supply of energy and Yippity is *slightly* faster than I am.

Every once in a while, I would randomly, and much to Yippity's surprise and delight, change the direction of the game. He would come sliding across the tiled kitchen floor where I would be waiting, I'd scoop him up into my arms, and he would lick my face until I let him go. You can imagine, Dear Reader, that this is pure joy to a young boy. Anyway, one time, I misjudged the turn-around point. I was running as fast as I could and intended to change direction to try to catch Yippity off guard. Instead of stopping, I tripped forward over a throw rug and at top speed, dove head-first into the corner of a brick wall.

At first, the collision between my skull and the corner of the brick wall didn't faze me. I knew I ran into it. My head was vibrating but there was no pain. Meanwhile, I did have the sense that there was some other stimuli that the rest of the house was reacting to. My head had connected with the wall so violently, that it literally caused the house to vibrate. I heard the step-grandpa, "What the hell was that?!!" To that question, my first thought was, 'oh no. I'm going to get in trouble'. With that, and in somewhat of a delirium by that moment, I went running into the living room where everyone was watching television.

My brain was starting to acknowledge the collision and the pain was setting in in an intense wave yet I was still silent and calm in this moment. My left eye went momentarily blind from the pain and even the lights were hurting me. I held a hand over the spot that collided with the wall as though it would diminish the pain. The ladies of the house were fretting. What to do. What to do. Finally, the grandmother spoke. "Gavi, let me see. Let me see". I removed my hand from my head and felt a warm trickle of fluid run down over my blind eye, down my cheek, and into my

146

mouth. It continued to drip. I put my hand back up to the spot on my head, pulled it down, and the fluid was clear.

The clear fluid, apparently, trickling out of my head, threw me into a frenzy. Now it was too much. I was screaming and crying and quite honestly, I was scared and relinquishing control to the pain. I gave into it and there was nothing else. To stop the leaking, the grandmother threw a towel around my head and tightened it. It seemed to work. We all made our way to the car, and before I knew it, we were in an emergency room with doctor's evaluating my condition. The doctor in charge, who was draped with red hair and a large, red beard, informed my mother, with me in the room, that I would need five stitches; three deep and two superficial. It's true, I remember these words exactly; these being deep and superficial with adjective-descriptor numbers. I didn't know what "superficial" meant and started crying uncontrollably. In my mind, superficial probably meant brain evisceration.

The doctor explained it all to me in lies like good doctors do to calm their young patients. The procedure was going well until he pulled out a lengthy hypodermic syringe. He forgot to mention he was going to inject lidocaine around the affected area so that I wouldn't feel the stitches. Once he explained it to me, I calmed down and let him proceed without any further delays. I didn't really feel the deep stitches but I most certainly felt the superficial ones and while he was running those through my skin and making his knots, I let out a few more quiet tears.

At the end of the procedure, he told me I was a brave, little boy and that I did well through the procedure. I was gleaming, but I also thought I would be in trouble with both the biological mother and *her* and I started to worry about it. When we got back to the biological mother's house, I took a look at the place where my head collided with the wall. I hit the wall so hard that I left some of my forehead skin behind. I peeled it off the corner and dangled it in front of me like string cheese. Also, I hit it so hard, that I broke a piece of the brick right out of the corner. I picked it up off the floor and handed it to the biological mother. She responded with, "What do you want me to do with it?". I didn't entertain a discussion about it. I threw it away.

That night it was really difficult to sleep. The lidocaine wore off and my head was throbbing intensely. The doctor told me I might have some headaches for a few weeks while my cerebrospinal fluid replenished itself. I never did bleed. I only leaked CSF from my skull and that's what the warm, clear fluid was. He also happened to mention there "shouldn't be any permanent damage".

In the morning, the biological mom came into the room and told me to pack my bag, that I was going home.

Gavi. I can't take care of you like this. It's too much work. It's...too hard. You've stressed me out so now you have to go home. Cheryl and your father can take care of you. You'll be fine there. You understand, right Gavi?

No. Not really. I'm feeling better, mom. See?

I got out of bed. I wasn't moving as fast as normal, but I felt like I could still have a good time. I could still listen and make mix tapes and pet the dogs. That was the end of the conversation though.

Pack your bag. I've called you father and let him know what happened. We're leaving in 15 minutes.

So...in dejected fashion, I packed my bag. I felt responsible, guilty, and ashamed. I know now, I had no reason to feel this way.

The stitches dissolved within three weeks and my head healed nicely save for the scar, that at 37 years old, is still noticeable. This was one of the last times I saw her in person and I was left with that feeling of how, this adult, the person supposedly responsible for me, couldn't help me or see this through to the end, because it was too hard, because I caused too much stress.

I couldn't have been more than 10 or 11 years old when I ran my head into that brick wall. The next time I saw her in person, I was in my early twenties, maybe twenty-three, had completed a tour in the U.S. active Army and was actively pursuing my Bachelor of Science in Sports Medicine Physiology at Eastern Michigan University – Go Eagles. Post-Script: They were formerly known as the Hurons, and while I attended EMU, there were still remnants of the Native American mascot.

My dad called me up and informed me that my biological grandmother, on my mother's side had passed away. He had no emotional response as he presented the news. It was all very matter of fact.

Gavi. Your mother's mother, that being your grandmother, has passed away. The family wanted you to know.

You might be wondering why the family just didn't pass this little nugget of information to me directly. Before I left home for the military, which was just two weeks after graduating high-school, I respectfully asked the parental units if they could respect a rule or two. One of the main rules was that if anyone from my past, to include the biological mother, wanted to be in touch with me, that they should take down their name, number, and when convenient, the parental units could call me with this information so that I could decide if I wanted to speak to whoever was trying to reach out. Let me tell you, this saved me from unnecessary drama throughout my young, adult life on more than several occasions. You see, I had a lot of girlfriends in high-school, not in an inappropriate sense, but in an emotional sense, and many of them still wanted to be emotionally connected to me. I had moved on.

I responded to my dad.

Ok, Dad. I'm not sure what to say or do. Do you think I should pay my respects? Are you planning to pay any respects?

I'm not planning to pay my respects. As you know Gavi, there's quite a bit of history there and for me, it's good riddance. May God damn her devil-heart to hell!

Jesus, Dad. Okay, but what do you think about my situation?

Yeah, I mean, I think it would be okay to pay your respects. You should probably do it.

My current boss has recently described me as a "man who is all things right and just". I am in Quality, afterall. Even in my early twenties, I had this highly tuned conscience of what was morally right and wrong. It's actually one good trait I can sincerely say came from my Christian upbringing (although I was never a

151

Subscriber), my grandma's wooden spoon, and my love of Batman comics.

I felt it was the right thing to do and decided to dutifully pay my respects.

In my personal life during this time I had suffered some recent setbacks. I was highly respected in the military and had made friends and high rank equally as fast. I left the military to pursue my education. When I left, I didn't just leave behind friends, rank, and respect, but I also left behind a fiancé of three years and also my confidence.

My first job after the military was a stock-boy for Toys 'R' Us which lasted all of three weeks. My second job after the military was a Manager for Dunham's, a sporting goods store which lasted for the duration of my undergrad pursuit. I dated a flurry of girls during this time and noticed that I was very attractive to older women, but hardly attractive to the demographic I was most interested in – twenty-somethings.

One of my buddies sarcastically pointed out the reasons: I was furry, short, and balding. I thought about this for a while. I can take care of furry. I can't take care of short. I explored options to take care of balding and found a solution. I went to a hair center for men, was examined, and was told that for a meagerly sum of

$12,500, I could have a new head of hair, *that would absolutely be my own hair growing from my scalp*. The details of this part of the story are actually much more involved, Dear Reader, trust me, but I am trying to provide some context for this, the definitive chapter on the biological mother. Anyway, as any young, desperate-for-love, testosterone-laden, blue-balled college-aged male, knows, you just have to have pussy and having a full head of hair is pre-requisite to that end. So, I agreed to the procedure, placed the full amount onto a credit card, and for $12,500, I received exactly 2500 of my own hair follicles surgically implanted into my scalp. I had this procedure only a week before my mother's mother had passed. Believe me, I deeply contemplated not paying my respects simply because my scalp was a scabbed mess of pus.

It was early spring when the funeral was being held. It was cold, and I was dressed appropriately. I wore pseudo-Sunday best and due to the weather, wore a cold-climate skull cap. I parked my truck and calmly, collectively and casually made my way to the front door.

On the front step, there *she* was. I recognized her instantly. My biological mother was on the step smoking a cigarette. She was heavier than I remember, but otherwise unmistakable. I walked up to her and said:

Hello. I'm very sorry for your loss.

Note, Dear Reader, not "Hello *mom*, I'm very sorry for your loss".

She looked at me. She looked me right in the eyes. Took another drag from her disgusting cigarette, exhaled into the cool night and said callously:

I'm sorry. Do I know you?

What did I really expect? She hadn't seen me grow up. Over 12 years had passed and her last visual memory of me was a scared, little boy getting stitches. Deep down, I think that I would expect a mother to recognize her son and I stood there, strangely disappointed. I gathered my oats.

Yes, I'm your son. I've come to pay my respects to your mother.

Michael?

I unexpectedly laughed and sarcastically commented back.

Um, yes. Unless you have another son? Ok, want to go inside?

We proceeded inside and unfortunately, I cannot fully recall the venue. I couldn't tell you if we were in some secular house or some funeral home. That detail does not fully matter. What I do remember is feeling very small amongst high ceilings and a massive crowd; with no one I recognized. What I do remember is taking a lot of deep breaths (always remember to be a gentleman; you're here to pay your respects; and for this moment in time that's all that matters!).

The biological mother and I walked to up her mother's casket. We stopped at the natural barrier to such proceedings. Chills ran up and down my spine. I was looking at her mother and my mother was staring at me. Wide-eyed, fixated staring. Now might be a good time to mention that I have bird-like peripheral vision! I see *everything* and I'm sure there will be a volume dedicated to my proven superpowers and until then Dear Reader, you'll just have to wait with baited anticipation. To be totally honest I did not know of the circumstances of my mother's mother's death and what was very eerie for me was that she looked exactly as when I had last visited which was the time I received those stitches in my head. Ironic that I'm visiting again at a moment on the planet when my head is healing from something.

As I said, my biological mother was staring at me. She started to breathe heavily. Longer than expected inhalations followed by a fast exhalation. It was so visibly noticeable that someone from the audience approached and asked us if we were ok. I was very happy to recognize this person. It was Aunt Billy. I responded, "Hey Aunt Billy. It's nice to see you. It's been a long time. We're fine for right now; we'll be with you in a few". Aunt Billy didn't recognize me. And that's ok, except she was the sane and cool one; As you'll come to see I could have really used an ally at this event. My voice seemed to pull the biological mother out of her trance and she quickly threw an arm around me. I almost screeched because it was fast and unexpected but I was able to keep it in. My heart beats per minute must have immediately doubled because I swear I could hear my heartbeat in my ears. I still have night terrors from what happened next.

Thinking of the antagonist in Stephen King's, "Misery", (and the movie version antagonist and my biological mother do look alike, Dear Reader, for the love of god!) the biological mother Vulcan neck-pinched me to turn me towards the direction of the massive crowd. The crowd, simply there to pay their respects had noticed a certain buzz teeming through the airwaves and like zombies had plodded their way methodically closer to the casket. If you were fully attuned to the atmosphere like I am and was in that moment, then you'd catch faint phrases and mutterings all referring to me such as: "Who is that?" "What's happening up there?" "Who's Yvonne with?". Having forced me into the position of her desire, and with me with an onset of dread, she proceeded, and to this day, Dear Reader, this became one of the most humiliating public experiences of my life – definitely worse than Mr. B teaching me that life lesson so many years ago.

So, there we are standing like duet singers in front of a buzzing audience at a dearly departed's funeral. The biological mother releases her release, turns to the audience and says somewhat duplicitously:

Hello everyone. It's so nice of all of you to pay your respects to MY mother. Gosh, it must be eons since I've seen some of you. As you know, I've been in the painstaking care of my mother ever since Leo, my asshole of a stepfather passed away. Billy, looks like I'm coming your way next. (She gave Aunt Billy a wink. Aunt Billy had the "oh shit" look on her face). *Anywho. We have a special guest with us tonight who I am certain was not actually invited. I guess we can thank my piece of shit ex-husband and his man-wife for that.* (She cackled. She was so delighted to have this moment, I think). *I wanted to introduce you to Gavino.* And with game-show-host-face and the adroit game show gesture she bleated: *He's my son.*

She paused for dramatic effect. There wasn't a sound. Time seemed to stop (for me) for a light year. Then, in stereo unison, the crowd exclaimed: "YOU HAVE A SON!". It roared and for a moment I was lost.

Then, the training from grandma as well as all of my training for the many Soldier of the Month boards I won, kicked in. I took a deep and centering breath, and new exactly what I needed to do and say next.

Thank you for having me everyone. (gratitude) I recognize only a few of you from the few times I was able to visit when Yvonne was lucid and accountable enough to have me over. (dig) I apologize that I do not recognize more of you. (contrition) If it hasn't been mentioned yet, there are refreshments and pastries over on the counter as you walked in. (customer service) The service will be getting started soon and if you'd like to pay your respects or fit a restroom break in now would be the time. (urgency) As for me, I have paid my respects and wish you all well; Thank you. (chivalry)

And that Dear Reader is my personal recipe for success for any moment that requires political savviness. □

I then turned to Yvonne, took a step forward to meet her eye to eye, and said, "I guess that didn't go the way you thought it would, huh?" She turned bright red and was about to go apeshit.

Instead Aunt Billy walked up, grabbed Yvonne by the arm, gave me a wink, and walked Yvonne to her seat.

As for me, I walked out the same way I came in and I never once looked back. Good riddance.

I would be remiss if I did not mention Dear Reader, that I maintained a pretty healthy and joyful disposition through my childhood and into adulthood. I am fairly certain that we have my grandma to thank for that who convinced me at an early age to "always wear a smile; don't let anyone know they got to you. You win that way, Gavi". Anyway, a decade elapsed and I have hardly ever put much thought into that event. All things considered it is a blip in time compared to a whole life to lead. I'm not sure what really bothered me more about that event. The fact that no one in an entire family remembered that I existed or that my biological mother did not recognize me. Again, I say that I didn't put much thought into it and my therapist would disagree! She would say something to the affect that you "never took time to grieve and as such your mind and body process this distress through night terrors". Fair enough Doc. As The Revisionist, I can take creative license here to say, I did grieve, rather I was able to get closure.

And as that decade elapsed I get a call from my dad, which, by the way, I can count on my two hands the number of times my dad or *her* have called me. (Asshole!). Always on my birthday. (gee thanks for the gift Asshole!). And only when someone has expired.

Hey Gavi. I hope you're ok. I have some news, rather good or bad, for you, I don't know. But for me, hallefuckinglujah, Yvonne passed away!

I received the news as much as you might expect if you're still reading at this point Dear Reader. Very factually without emotion as though I were in a meeting at work while someone is presenting facts and figures from PowerPoint slides.

Ok, thanks for the update Dad.

I'm sorry Gavi, there's more.

Ok, what else?

Well, I haven't been in touch with the wackadoodles for a very long time. I have just been paying for all the medical bills per the courts orders from yesteryear so on and so forth. And anyway, this Lady leaves a voicemail on our landline. She let us know that there is a lawyer (or some similar person) trying to reach you because you are the next of kin and there is some, uh, final acts that need some signatures from those who are legally obligated to act given this circumstance. So, we have an agreement Gavi, and

I've honored it here. I have not provided this Lady with your phone number. What do you want me to do?

Go ahead and give it to her. I'm next of kin huh?

Are you fucking kidding me? I'm next of kin and I am legally obligated to do whatever the fuck is going to happen next. Please realize Dear Reader, at this point in time, I'm married to DoYoung, and we are living our best life in Long Beach, California. Yvonne's death occurred in Detroit, Michigan. It is quite inconvenient and expensive to travel from California and Michigan and then back. Those were my first thoughts. And then, I came back to Earth and became Mr. Obligation. Of course it is my responsibility. Of course I will take care of it. My Dad and Cheryl were so very happy that they no longer had to have this financial responsibility and I don't blame them.

Anyway, DoYoung and I made travel arrangements and we thought we would make a little vacation out of it too and visit all of our Michigan friends. However, as soon as we touched down, this kind of melancholy came over me. I had some serious business to complete here and that's how we ended up treating the trip: like business. I don't regret that at all even though it would end up being the last opportunity we would make to travel to Michigan.

Thinking about how to portray this next part of the story, and after writing those last two paragraphs, I remembered that I kept a copy of the form I had to sign for the Funeral Home to release my biological mother's body and other such next steps, for now, let's say the final resting place and so on and so forth. I'm a pretty organized guy so I went and looked for the form in the archives. Instead of finding the form I found a little notebook that I had taken with me to help us stay organized for the trip. Inside of the notebook it had all of the glorious details: Where we stayed, what flights we took, who, what, when, where, how much and how many in other words. That would be the 4W2H method of collecting and analyzing data by the way. □ And, I had arranged little post it notes within the spiral notebook to keep track of other details worth recording. After seeing post-it notes contained within the spiral notebook I remembered that I had accidentally left the notebook behind when we had left the hotel for a related outing and DoYoung and I stopped at Office Depot to buy a post-it note pad so that we could keep track of any important subjects. I have purged most of the details from my memory actually, and what you'll read next will be courtesy of those post-it notes.

I received the contact name and number for Vick's Funeral Home in Mt. Clemens Michigan. I worked with Mary who was very sweet and for some reason was suspicious of me as she was always raising her left eyebrow anytime I spoke to her. I think she remembered me from Lutheran High School North as a punk ass trouble maker – that is how I was perceived and well, perception is reality even if it is inaccurate. Mary was fine enough to work with and informed me that I had a lot of steps to complete. I quickly realized I would not be able to do this next of kin thing alone. DoYoung recently had received notice that she had passed the California Bar exam so I tapped DoYoung for some legal advice and some critical thinking. Together we came up with a list of questions for all parties involved. As we would come to learn, there was the funeral home party, Aunt Billy and her daughter Mercedes, and Alex who "technically" was Yvonne's "guardian" from the group home that Yvonne had lived in for greater than 2 years, and finally my dad.

The questions:

1. Is there a will? Is there an estate that needs to be settled?

2. Are there any personal artifacts I might be interested in?

3. Where was she living? Are there things there that might be released to me?

4. Were there any lucid moments that I might know more about over the past few years?

5. Based on whatever final resting options are available, how will this be funded?

6. Does Yvonne's immediate family members (Aunt Billy, her sister) have any preferences?

7. Is there anything Yvonne asked you to say to me or to give to me?

8. Is there any money?

9. Is there any property?

10. Dad, do you want to see the body, you know, for closure or something?

Now, who answered which questions is not a matter of importance as far as I'm concerned Dear Reader, except for that last one. To which my Dad simply restated, "Thanks but no fucking way".

One at a time then, shall we?

1. Is there a will? Is there an estate that needs to be settled? No.

2. Are there any personal artifacts I might be interested in?

This question was first answered by Aunt Billy. I learned that Aunt Billy was her "technical" guardian and that Aunt Billy tried to handle crazy (wackadoodles) and realized, and rightly so if you ask me, that it was not her responsibility. She arranged for Yvonne a group home to live in. My Dad had provided me Aunt Billy's phone number in the event that I wanted to discuss any of the details with her. I did, actually, so I called her up.

Gavi, it's very nice to hear from you. I want to start off immediately by saying I was super proud of you at my mother's funeral. I thought you handled it very well and I don't blame you for walking out straight away.

I welled up with a tear. Gravity took over from there and it slid ever so deliberately down the rest of my face and fell to the floor. I don't understand why that had such an impact and there was a certain relief (closure) about it I suppose.

Thank you Aunt Billy. I really do appreciate that. I'm sorry for your loss. I hope it was ok, but my dad gave me your number and if you're up for it, I have a few questions. I'm, you know, next of kin, and I'm trying to settle Yvonne's affairs. I'm here in Michigan with my wife and have a few tasks at hand to complete. And also, I'm a little curious about some specific things.

I understand Gavi. Yes, of course. I'm up for it and fire away. You know, if you were up for it, you could come visit me and my daughter and we could sort through it together.

Well, ok, let me get through some questions now and then if we can find time with all that is needed to be completed I think that would be ok. (I actually didn't think it would be okay and my mind raced back to a time where I was firing a loaded .38 in downtown Detroit – "wackadoodles").

Sure Gavi. I'll provide any information that I can.

I asked her question number 2 from above and it was really the only question I needed to ask Aunt Billy.

Gavi, after my mother passed away, and I hate to say this, but Yvonne was right. I was the next in line to be her guardian. I did it for a time and she actually moved in with me for a while. It was ok to start. You know she was starting to have more lucid moments than not and for a while it was great to have my sister again. I don't know if you know this detail but she was a normal woman prior to having you, sorry, that's no judgment to you or to Manlio. Anyway, like I said it was good to have my sister again. It was like old times. That was until I came home from work one day and walked in on her giving my husband a blow job while he was finger banging her. It was traumatic back then and funny now. Mercedes and I have a wonderful life without both of those assholes anyway! I kind of knew he was stepping out on me and had no idea it was with my schizophrenic sister. The look on their faces when I caught them. Anyway, after that I divorced him and kicked him out of the house. It took a few months but I eventually

166

found an affordable group home for Yvonne to live in. Apparently there are many houses in Detroit set up like this so that families like ours can have respite from their mentally ill siblings. I set her up in a group home and within a week I received a call from the home director indicating that Yvonne had run away. She was nowhere to be found. To be honest Gavi, the first time I had heard of how my sister was doing since way back then was when a hospital nurse called me to inform me that she had passed in the night from a massive cardio event. The nurse gave me the number to an Alex who for the past two years was Yvonne's caretaker in a group home in Detroit. It was a different one than the one she had run away from of course. I guess, in some regard, I was relieved that she was "somewhere" the past few years vs homeless on the streets of inner city Detroit, or worse, some crack-house whore-house, or, uh, you know, dead in a ditch. And as they say, most folks prefer the "heart attack method" vs the "cancer method". So, I'd recommend you call this Alex and I'll give her number to you in a moment. One more thing Gavi. I did go to the home and collected a few of Yvonne's belongings. There wasn't much there. And she still did have some jewelry from our childhoods. It's pretty sentimental to me and I would very much like to keep these few pieces in remembrance of her. It wasn't all bad don't cha know. I also grabbed her purse, IDs, credit cards, and other little trinkets.

She paused for my response and I responded without hesitation and also without a follow up question.

Of course Aunt Billy.

Gavi, the only other item I should mention here is that you should have really low expectations if you're planning to visit the home. Are you planning to do that Gavi?

I again responded without hesitation.

Yes, I plan to make a visit and settle whatever affairs that I'm obligated to complete. And also, I am curious. I would like to talk with Alex. You know Aunt Billy, it was not an easy childhood with both Yvonne and Cheryl as primary and leading female figureheads in my life. DoYoung thanks the stars every night for Grandma. I don't want to say too much here out of respect for your loss but I basically have abandonment issues from Yvonne and I'm sure you remember *her*. This journey, for me Aunt Billy, although it started as an obligation has become psychologically meaningful for me and I think I'm really here because The Universe wants me to close out this chapter of my life. It has been an uncertain and a lingering aspect hanging over me for many years. I can tell you that on occasion, rare, I have thought of her from time to time. Like you said, it wasn't all bad. A fond memory that I hold onto is making those mix tapes hoping that the radio station would put on a Michael Jackson track.

At that moment, I heard Aunt Billy let out a deep sigh. Then, I think we were both collecting our thoughts silently. Most deep conversations have a natural lull every twenty minutes. Science says this is because it's time for our predator brain to become silent, look around, and inspect that we're not being preyed upon.

Enough said Gavi. Understood. I'll text you Alex's address and phone number. Good luck on your journey and if you need any help with anything please do let me know. We don't have a lot of money Gavi and we're relying on you to finalize everything. We'd prefer you don't do anything special. I said my goodbye when I viewed her at the hospital.

Then, just like that, she hung up. I think I was offended back then and reflecting on it now it was probably for the best. What else was there to ask of Aunt Billy? I reflected on all that we had discussed, caught DoYoung up who mostly was a silent listener for nearly all of this journey. Then the text came in with the details and from our hotel room and I made my next call to Alex and I'm glad that I did.

After the first ring she picked up.

Hello Alex. My name is Gavino Donato. You may recognize my last name as I understand you were Yvonne Donato's caretaker. (P.S. Dear Reader, why she chose to keep the last name will forever be lost to time). I'm her son.

To which she replied, "Yvonne had a son??!!?".

Dear Reader, that is a cruel joke at your behest but I am The Revisionist. What she really said was…

Hello Gavino. I've been expecting your call actually and your Aunt Billy let me know that someone with a Californian area code would be calling me soon. As she explained it to me she said you have some questions. I'd be happy to answer any questions you have and I'll do my best and help wherever I can. I'm sorry for your loss.

I'm sorry for yours Alex. As her caretaker, were you close to Yvonne?

No, not really Gavino.

Please, call me Gavi.

Uh, ok, sure thing Gavi. I don't know if you know much about the caretaking business so maybe I should provide a little context to that end. As a caretaker, I did have a relationship with your mother but only really on a check in basis. I own a home. In that home there are several bedrooms and each person I care for has a bedroom, a shared bathroom with others in the home, and a shared kitchen. We're not really a family and instead we're a routine. We're a, uh, schedule of events with a regimented calendar. The calendar is in place sort of like a Bed & Breakfast where breakfast, lunch, and dinner are all scheduled events. In the interim periods there are medicines to administer and also ensuring the medicines are consumed. It's a full time job Gavi that many fine folks like yourself aren't in the know about such things. And it's set up that way on purpose. Obviously her immediately family could not find it within themselves to care for her.

Thanks for the fucking dig there Alex. If only you knew the details contained herein.

I see, thank you for the explanation. Would it be possible to meet with you in person? And would it also be possible to see where Yvonne was living? I'm also asking if there are any belongings left behind that I might be able to take off of your hands.

Seconds ticked by. There wasn't even any background noise. It was eerie.

I don't think stopping by is an option. That said, I am happy to describe the conditions if you'd like. Also, Yvonne didn't have anything that you would be interested in. Just some old, tattered clothing. Your Aunt Billy already picked up anything of substance such as a purse and her IDs. If you're asking about money, all she had was $50.00 in a savings account. That's the other thing about caretaking; the money comes from your mother's social security checks. As it is, it barely covered her expenses.

This made me want to ask about what exactly did my asshole of a dad and *her* cover then? I let it go.

The expenses went to renting the room, food, the community kitchen and her health care such as prescriptions and hygiene. I think you get it.

Thank you Alex. Is there anything you can tell me about Yvonne? I mean, did she have a routine? Did she have any friends? What was her life like?

Are you sure you want to know this?

Alex, I had a very difficult childhood. Without going into too much detail I believe this will be my last opportunity to understand anything about anything that has happened in the past. I'm hoping you can afford me not more than 30 minutes of your time and then

I promise, you won't hear from me again. I just have a few things on my mind and really this is my last chance to have any closure on this topic. It's been lingering for me for years. Yvonne and I both made this decision, whether lucid on her part or not, I don't know and I don't think that really matters any longer. I would just really appreciate a few more minutes. Please.

Dear Reader, that "please" was stated matter of fact. It was not desperate. It was not a question either. Alex now had an opportunity to say fuck off and hang up or understand it was more of a directive. Dealer's choice.

I will give you the 30 minutes and the clock starts right now. Yvonne lived a quiet life. She mostly kept to herself. She liked to make plastic jewelry and hand it out to the other residents. She ate a lot. Did not move around much. And she drank a lot too. I'm sorry. I think you should prepare yourself if you're planning to "view" her.

Noted. Thank you.

And then the strangest question entered my mind. I'm glad it did. I hesitated in asking it and it ended up rolling out of my mouth like vomit and I had an emotional outburst that did end up sounding desperate.

Did she ever talk about me?

She did. Many a night would she break down in tears and in a dreadfully awful sobbing voice would let out a "MY SON!!". She never discussed with me in any detail what the origin of the outburst was, how it made her feel, or what it actually meant. She would say she didn't want to talk about it and that she did understand why you wouldn't want to be in touch with her. She told me once that she didn't blame you. She did love you Gavi. No matter what you think happened or not. She did love you. That's fucking biology there dude!

At this point I was crying uncontrollably. My thirty minutes was ticking away. I think Alex let me have this moment for approximately 5 minutes. That is a lifetime, on a phone, with a stranger. "Gavi, if there is nothing else..." I took a deep breath.

Ok. Yes, there is something else. Did she ever remarry or have any boyfriends or significant others? Did she have any friends? Is there anything else you can think of that I might like to know?

Solid open-ended question, thank you Root Cause Analysis Training.

There is actually. She had a hard life Gavi. She moved from home to home to home. She was with me for two years. I think it was probably the longest stead in her life other than when her mother and stepfather were her guardians. I never saw her with any boyfriends if she had any. And no, frankly, she did not have any friends. She was lonely. She was always lost within herself. The only time she was lucid was the few times she made those little trinkets I mentioned. My residents have hardly ever received any visitors. These folks are lost and forgotten. No matter what their circumstance you have to admit on some level that it is horrible to be rejected by your loved ones. Oh, last thing and our time is up. There was a picture of a baby taped to her mirror. She would stare at it sometimes for hours at a time always crying. I know for a fact it is not a picture of you. I don't know who it is of. She would never tell me no matter how many times I asked. Goodbye Mr. Donato. Do not ever call me again.

Click.

What the actual fuck? My mind flashed back to, "Michael", "Yes, unless you have another son..." Regardless, I was finally feeling some empathy for Yvonne. And also Alex was profound in her note on how horrible it is to be rejected by your loved ones. I can relate. I know exactly how that feels. I honored my commitment to Alex and I did not call her ever again.

175

Reflecting back on the questions on this journey I realized that nearly all were answered. There was no will. There was no estate that needed to be settled. There were no personal artifacts that I was interested in. I determined where she was living. There was nothing to be released to me. There was some crazy baby picture and no one knows who the baby was. The few lucid moments were spent lamenting about me and making plastic jewelry. There was no money and no property. So, what was left was the final resting place and the body itself.

In parallel to the time spent with Aunt Billy and Alex, DoYoung had helped me by making some arrangements to have Yvonne transferred to Vick's Funeral Home. I had been contemplating the whole trip if I should see Yvonne. I was asking everybody for advice. Most chose to remain silent. I don't blame them. This is kind of a unique situation. What I mean is I know I'm not the only one ever that has been in this position but with my immediate network I definitely was the only one to date put in this position. I eventually decided that I needed to see Yvonne one last time, you know, for closure or something. And for $100 Mary let me have a private viewing for 15 minutes. She did so begrudgingly and with a visible galling attitude I might add. Fuck you Mary.

On January 17th of the year 2015 I saw Yvonne for the last time.   Nothing except horror movies can prepare you for something like this.

When someone is found dead, an ambulance or an EMT crew in a minivan arrives to the residence, examines the corpse, and confirms the individual has in fact expired. Then, the body is placed on a stretcher, covered, and transferred from the place of death to a funeral home. Of course if you still have a pulse then you're transferred to a hospital. Then, at the funeral home the arrangements are made by, can you guess Dear Reader, the next of fucking kin. I did end up respecting Aunt Billy's request of "please don't do anything".

For cases like Yvonne, the funeral home will meet the minimum requirements of the codes or laws of the state and county for the cadaver. For the city of Mt. Clemens it meant that Yvonne was placed into a coffin-shaped box made of pine. It's the cheapest material and it burns quickly and it does not contain metal.

Vick's funeral home had placed Yvonne in a small staging area. The lid to the casket was uncovered to such a degree that only her face could be seen. I realized too late that this was because she was naked. And also the staging room was the room where bodies go to be cremated. I had asked DoYoung to please remain outside of the staging area and that I'd call for her if I needed anything.

It took me a few moments to gain any confidence to enter that room. I didn't know what to expect. This was uncharted territory. My heart was racing. Mary snootily reminded me that I was on the clock. Fuck you Mary! I walked in and immediately began to sob. I had not expected that I would be emotionally impacted by this at all. I had expected that I would walk in, say what I needed to say, and that would be it, thanks so much. Everyone has a plan until they get punched in the face. And I was punched in the face.

The first thing I registered was the smell. Yvonne was "warm" for some time and her body was already decomposing. There was also the smell of cooked, dead flesh as Yvonne was staged next to the cremation vault and actually ready to go in. In a previous life I had learned of and tolerated the scent of autoclaved Rhesus monkeys and the cremation vault scent was by far way more disgusting. I almost vomited. Perhaps Mary was so snooty because I was constraining the final step of the process for Yvonne's remains which as I've stated were in-process of decomposing.

I realized in that moment that I needed some help. Dear Reader, I never need help just for some context on how profound of a realization that actually is. I called to DoYoung who came in and placed a reassuring hand on my shoulder followed by a warm embrace further followed by "I got you". I wept in that embrace for several seconds, collected myself, and finally traversed the cremation vault tiled floor and was at the head of her casket. DoYoung never said a word and I never needed her to. Her life-force presence brought balance to the presence of the deceased allowing my mind to center and calm myself.

I approached Yvonne like a whisper. I don't know why I felt like I needed to be so quiet and the best I can mutter now is that it was out of respect of the dead. If you think historically about how the definition of "dead" has changed over time, then the gentleman in me remains mindful that there could yet still be some life to some cell in that body. I think it is best to respect that in the event that cells are animated in such a manner that they can take their revenge on you should you choose to desecrate it. "Always be a gentleman".

In cases such as these, there is no mortuary work completed on the deceased. There's no make up, there's no embalming, nothing. There is just the rawness of the rigor mortis combined with the death event itself. Yvonne had had a massive cardiac arrest in her sleep, at night, and was not found dead until the middle of the morning the next day. The last time I had seen her in person was over a decade ago where she was not thin but she wasn't thick either. The second thing I registered was how morbidly obese Yvonne had become. No Revision here, she hardly was able to fit in the coffin-pine-box. I have to wonder while I write these words what kind of effort had to be made by the funeral home to get her in there. If I had to guess, I'd say she was easily 350lbs. She was obviously cyanotic. Her eyes were dull, one was translucent white, and the other was blood red as it had basically exploded from the pressure of the cardiac event. In any case, they were open and I struggled momentarily to look into those eyes one last time. Her hair was ratty. Her lips were purple and there was some fluid which I do not presume to know or want to think about what it was coming out of her mouth. Her pimpled right arm was propped up on her bloated stomach exposing a lifeless, stiff hand and purple finger tips. I was regretting this decision to view and for a long time all I could do was stare. Other than the cadaver lab in college, I have not had many encounters with the dead. I hope to keep it that way. I also knew my time and my opportunity for closure was evaporating.

I touched her cold hand. Which I had not expected was something that I would do. It was involuntary. And. There was nothing. There was finality. And identifying finality brought me a sense of inner peace. It was not the closure I was expecting. It was the closure I received. This is what the universe brought me. This, my biological mother, was now nothing and only a memory. I choose to believe that while you still think of someone, even if they are no longer tangibly here, that they are still actually here with you; still present. And if you choose that, you can also choose to let that have influence on you.

And with that, my inner dialogue provided a definitive conclusion.

You can't hurt me any more Yvonne. I will never think of you again. You no longer exist.

DoYoung and I walked out of the staging area where Mary's team were anxiously waiting to push Yvonne into the flames. I turned around, watched them shove her into the vault and watched the flames engulf the box and all of its contents.

Thank you for giving birth to me. We have an amazing life. Rest in peace.

Chapter 12

After the *closure* event, DoYoung and I made an obligatory visit to those that at that moment in time I still called the "Parental Units". Manlio and Cheryl greeted DoYoung and I at their front door. After the introductions and small talk subsided, Cheryl turned to me and said…

I can't believe you came here for her. We were not expecting that.

I needed closure. Also, I'm next of kin. That's not something that can be delegated.

And at that last word, "delegated", I knew the rest of the visit was going to go horribly wrong. Afterall, I had used a word with four syllables Cheryl was a one syllable gal after all. Two at most.

Come here. I want to show you something.

Already with her fucking directives. And already I was reminded of why I did not want to be here.

DoYoung and I hesitated, looked at each other, and telepathically agreed that together we would go and view the "something". Cheryl had pulled out several photo albums.

Unbeknownst to me throughout my entire childhood was that there were several photo albums of my dad's early life, before Cheryl (BC?) where there were many pictures of my dad, my biological mom, and me as a family unit. I hardly have memories of that time period. However, as I turned the pages of the album I did note that in many of them we all actually looked really happy. I arrived to a photo of just me and Yvonne. I took it out of the album. I studied it for a minute and just like that I was transported back in time to some proceeding involving lawyers and judges.

I remember feeling very small in a very large room. On one side of the room was my dad. On the other side of the room was Yvonne. I was in a chair in the middle and a man in a black cloak spoke to me. I was barely four years old at the time and I don't recall all of the details any longer but what I do remember is that there were long conversations between my dad and the man in the black cloak. There were long conversations between Yvonne and the man in the black cloak. And after what felt like forever to me, the man in the black cloak turned to me and I remember we spoke for a long time. Whatever my responses were made the man in the black cloak comfortable enough to ask me a specific question.

Gavi, you're a very smart boy. I've enjoyed our conversation today.

I smiled. I was so fucking cute back then with my dimpled left cheek and full head of hair.

I want to ask you a very important question. I don't want you to respond immediately to the question, ok, do you understand?

Yes sir.

Good. This question will determine how the rest of your life proceeds. It's that important! Again, take your time, really think hard before you respond. Ok? So here it is. I've heard both your father and your mother today. I can tell they both really love you. Unfortunately, I have to make a decision on who should have the primary rights to care for you. Now, that doesn't mean you're losing someone today. Not at all. What it means is, who will you stay with the most and also who will you visit but not live with. Ok? So...that's what we have to decide today.

So, Gavi, which one of your parents do you want to live with?

As I recall this memory right now Dear Reader, I have to be honest with you. I'm crying right now. Are you fucking kidding me? Four years old and I have to decide what parent I'm going to live with? I have to decide that!?! That still doesn't feel right to me that all the way back in this one moment barely able to ride a bike that it ended up being my decision for how the rest of my life would turn out.

I looked at Yvonne. She was desperately trying to telepathically have me lean towards her. I recall that both parents were not allowed to say anything in this moment. There was just the big, open room, and as far as I was concerned there was just now, me, my dad, and the biological mother. I started to fidget in my chair. I was staring at Yvonne. She was giving me looks and gestures trying to provoke me to say "yes". If I had to guess, I think she was very much looking forward to the day that I was more mature so that she could try to fuck me. I turned my gaze away from Yvonne and made eye contact with my dad. He was standing very calmly, with his hands relaxed at his sides. And, he was beaming, quite proudly that I was up there in the front of the room in this big chair, and at four, actually weighing out the pros and cons of who I should live with. If I were to ask him what he was thinking about at the time, I imagine it would go something like this:

Gavi, in that moment, I have to say that I was not expecting the Judge to put you in such a position. Your mother, as fucking crazy as she was, actually showed up and made a compelling argument. I did not expect that. I underestimated her there and so did my fucking lawyer. Speaking of that asshole, he didn't do a god damn thing for this and so here we are with our dicks in our hand. And as it turns out, it looks like the heavens have you determining your destiny. I was in shock and awe. I knew in my heart that you would make the right decision for you. I knew in this moment you would reflect back on the violence you had witnessed to your grandma. I knew you would think about the amazing time you had with your grandma, grandpa, and your cousins. And, I knew you'd recall how it was you came to be there and how I had to suddenly drive up to the UP and pick you up. I knew that at four you already had an old soul and I knew that your decision would reflect the insane life experiences that you were already exposed to. And most importantly, I know that you felt your dad's care and love for you way more than what you had experienced with your mother.

Yeah. Wow. He was right. I did think about all of those things.

I turned to the judge and emphatically said, "My dad. I wish to be with my dad". I wish I had been a smarter little boy because I would have offered a third option. Grandma and Grandpa.

And so it was. I asked Cheryl if I could have this photo that transported me back in time to this event. To which she begrudgingly agreed. I don't ever look at it these days because then

Yvonne would still be here with me and well, reflect back on the last chapter Dear Reader. And anyway we looked at the other photos and I reminisced with DoYoung on other events that I could recall. As I did so, Cheryl would butt in with some remark on some historical context or the name of some long and forgotten relatives on her side to which no one even acknowledged. Not even Manlio.

I have exactly one, and only one good memory of Cheryl. She once took me to Wendy's where I demolished a doubly stacked cheeseburger, seasoned fries, a coke, and a chocolate frosty. I was about 10 or so and it was one of the only times that I can recall where Cheryl wasn't trying to convince me that I should do something her way or think about something her way. We had a great time. I imagine today she thinks about that event quite often. The rest of the memories are shit. And as I later learned through therapy could be classified as abuse. At the time, I just thought all of it was normal; that everyone experiences what I went through. And also to be fair, I wasn't the easiest kid to raise, however, I was a kid and she was an adult and I know even with her low intellectual acuity that she knew what she did was wrong.

I am now going to have to admit, that between the ages of 3-7 years old, I often wet the bed in the middle of the night. This is medically known as nocturnal enuresis and is a result of having a small bladder, sleep apnea, and stress and anxiety. Bingo. That last one. As a young boy, dealing with the trauma of the violence I was a witness too and also now being forced to have a new "mom" in my life, forced to call her mom, and also the great rigor and pressure that Cheryl put on me every day and every night, of course I was wetting the bed. Because bedwetting was occurring way after I was potty trained and at 7 years old my parents took me to see a doctor.

The doctor diagnosed me as having a small bladder. Obviously he was not aware of the historical context and so he prescribed a moisture alarm and advised my parents on how to help me work on my bladder size. Now, the moisture alarm is a small, battery operated device that basically connects an electrical circuit with the moisture from urine when you urinate and then sounds an alarm so that the child can either wake up and stop the flow of urine or so that a parent can hear it, run into the room, wake the child up so that the child can prevent any further flow and therefore make it to the bathroom.

What they don't tell you in the literature is that the device is literally a clamp which clamps to the head of the penis. For those who have a penis, they know that the head is very sensitive and the device was very painful. Depending on your seven year old penis size it certainly is not a one size fits all situation. And for seven, I guess I had a pretty good sized penis and of course a circumcised one. I'm not bragging here and this is not my ego, but when the doctor examined my genitalia, which he did from a kneeling position, he had quite a surprised look on his face when I pulled my pants down and well, you know, there it was dangling in front of him. Anyway, what they also don't tell you is that in fact there is an electrical shock to your penis head when the circuit is completed. I hope Dear Reader, this sounds medieval to you, because that's how it still feels to me today. It was all very uncomfortable situation and also very painful. And that's not even the worse of it.

It wasn't my dad who would install the device every night, it was Cheryl. (Although, I do remember he did it a few times).

Cheryl would saunter her way into my bedroom and every fucking night she had a shit eating grin on her face. She looked forward to installing the device, I'm certain of it. And for a quick reminder of what this woman looks like, think of an elderly Hillary Clinton. Then, in a sultry cookie monster voice…

Ok Gavi. You know what time it is. I want you to stand up now. I want those pants to come off. Do it. I want to watch you By the way you little shit, your penis is nothing compared to your dad's. Oh my god his penis is so fucking big. It fills me up Gavi.

And when you're a little older, you're going to fill me up too! You just wait.

I was very scared of this woman. In a recent conversation with one of my cousins I grew up with at grandma's place, my cousin reminded me of how whenever Cheryl was around, I was nervous, that I clammed up, and was a perfect little adult. And whenever Cheryl was not around, that I was a very relaxed and fun Gavi. Anyway because of my fear I was almost always compliant. This woman had at least 100 lbs on me and at this time, she was also still very muscular from her days of softball, bowling, and practicing with a bow. During these episodes of installing the device, I never said a word for fear of my life and also for the fear of provoking her to inflict harm on me. Afterall my dad was ok with this (*Asshole!*)

When my pants were off, and when I stood there naked, afraid, and vulnerable, she would get on her knees and lean in towards me. She would grab my penis by the shaft with her palm of one of her manly sized hands, apply sexual pressure and would stroke me.

Do you feel this Gavi? Does this feel good Gavi? Oh, it must feel good. Do you see that you're getting bigger. That's such a good boy! I wonder if I could make you cum. Do you want to cum Gavi? Oh god!

She would also often place her face close to my penis. Now, I'll go ahead and state resolutely that the installation of the device never resulted in fellatio. Thank the universe because I think I would have turned into a psychopath serial killer. That said, she would lean in and blow cool air on my penis. This would go on for minutes and after a while, my dad started to suspect something although he never ever directly confronted either of us. I don't blame him for that actually. He would call out sometimes, "what's taking so long in there?". Yes, exactly, I do wish he had walked in on it because it would have saved me a childhood of agony.

She would put the clamp on my penis and tuck me in. Then she would kiss me full on the lips and also put her fucking tongue in my mouth and move it around a bit trying to find my tongue. I remember this all very distinctly because she had a severe case of halitosis from sipping coffee all day. It was funking rank in that mouth.

I love you Gavi. Don't you fucking wet the bed tonight. I'm all hot and bothered now and I'm going to go fuck your dad while I'm thinking about you. I'm going to cum so hard thinking about you. Don't fucking ruin it for me!

After the horrific event had concluded, I would often lay awake in bed for hours scared that she might come back and "fill her up" whatever the fuck that meant. I developed a super power as a result of this abuse which I'm still not ready to divulge to you Dear Reader. However, that said, I would take all of my stuft animal toys where I would proceed to have stuft animal martial arts fights. These fights would last for hours until I drifted off. Tigger would always win by the way!

As soon as I woke up in the mornings and to work on my bladder size, I was forced to drink several glasses of water in rapid succession. I would estimate three 8-ounce glasses. Then, I was told I was not allowed to use the bathroom for many hours no matter how badly I had to go. I was not allowed to micturate for any of the morning leading into the noon hour. And, anytime I was allowed to go, I was to be supervised by Cheryl. As part of this prescription my dad and Cheryl were advised that I was to work on my detrusor muscles.

The detrusor muscle contracts to push the urine out of the bladder and into the urethra so that the urine can make its great escape. That muscle will relax to allow the storage of the urine in the urinary bladder. And so, the doctor wanted me to develop that muscle as perhaps a reason that I was wetting the bed was that the muscle was weaker than it should be by my age. When it was time urinate, I was to only let out a little, hold it, and then let out a little more and so on and so forth and that is the reason I needed "supervision". And of course this task fell to Cheryl since my dad had to work and Cheryl was a stay at home "mom".

Again, I was a compliant little Gavi. Imagine if you will, the longest time you have ever had to hold your urine or feces when you have felt like you were already at your maximum capacity. Then, multiply that by a factor of 100 and you might be getting close to how I felt every day, twice a day for a duration I do not care to try to remember. It was at least a full summer.

For "supervison", Cheryl would take the same position and have the same disposition as that of our nightly "routine". The difference in the routine is that she would force the issue and try to control the rate of my evacuation. So, on her knees, she would grab my penis and by gripping it try to control the rate of my flow. She would squeeze me very hard to stop me from peeing and then would relax her grip to let me go again. I have sometimes wondered if this is what the doctor meant. In my research about this issue, I believe this was not the intent. I was to flex the muscle and relax the muscle. And a fucking death grip was not the correct course. And again, my therapist agrees and informed me that this too was a form of sexual abuse. Because also Cheryl would have similar disgusting things to whisper in my ear.

193

There was one time that I remember that I didn't care. I really had to go. And so actually, I pissed all over her hands and definitely some splashed on her face and clothes. I just let it all flow and as DoYoung is fond of reminding me that I have an "aggressive pee stream".

How fucking dare you! You fuck! You asshole!

hich was followed up with Cheryl punching me, repeatedly on my dick and nuts. When the punching was over, she slapped me everywhere on my whole body. As I think back on this, it suddenly occurs to me that I believe in this moment I was starting to become what I can only label as "aware". When I decided in that moment to let the urine flow, and in my mind I said, "let it go", it opened a door inside me. I realized I could take back my power. I realized that in my compliance that it actually made me helpless. And when I decided that I could have power, it changed me. I recognized in Cheryl an afraid and horrified face when I defied her instruction especially considering the end result was me literally pissing on her.

She was still on her knees and so I took it one step further and I pushed her hard enough for her to fall over. This made me realize I was actually a lot stronger than most folks would have considered given my short and skinny physique. I ran out of the

194

house and stayed out of the house until I was certain my dad was home from work.

And after that episode, I was no longer a bed wetter.

Now, I don't know if it's because of the device, the exercises, or me taking back my power. I would like to believe it's the latter. The three doctors that I've consulted with while writing this agree with me.

I know what I've written here is horrific. But it wasn't all doom and gloom. Ok, me being me, I made a game out of the exercise thing. For example, I would pretend that my dog needed to go outside and go potty. And in so doing, I would let her run around the yard while I actually had unzipped my jeans, let my dick out through the zipper opening, and would keep a normal standing position and would pee. Yep, right there in plain sight. What I've learned in my more recent years is that people are generally unaware 1) of themselves 2) of their surroundings and 3) of other people. When you're sneaking around is usually when you get caught. Our ancestor instincts suddenly go off like Spidey senses. And so, in order to remain inconspicuous, I literally pissed in plain sight. I'm laughing right now thinking about that and I hope you are too.

I did get caught once, and only once. I didn't think it all the way through and often I would run to the side of the house where no one could see me and I would pee as fast as I could. The problem was that I actually peed on the house leaving the moisture evidence there for Cheryl The Supervising Inspector to locate which she eventually did. I got the leather belt on my ass with 10 lashes for that. Yeah, my disobedience definitely required that level of punishment. (Asshole!) Moving on...

My dog was a dappled dachshund and was a very sweet girl. She was my best friend. We picked her up from some farm and from a licensed breeder. She was a pure bred and I had her from the time she was a small puppy and at a time when I could take full care of her. That was the agreement that my dad and I had made. We can get a dog so long as I was the full caretaker which meant training her, feeding her, and picking up her poop among other tasks. Her name was Penne. Yep, like the pasta. I had wanted to name her something more human such as Malissa or Jennifer and my dad explained to me that we give our pets non-human names. Sure dad. One day, while Penne was in her elderly years, and of course she was a very obedient dog and I trained her well including potty training, she began urinating in the house and frequently at that. She could not control it in time to notify me and to get outside in time. As pet lovers know, this is a sign that the dog has

196

developed doggy diabetes. Cheryl took Penne to the vet. She took Penne and left me at home.

And that was the last time I saw Penne.

Cheryl knew what the situation was because she had many dogs in her sordid lifetime. She planned ahead with the vet that Penne was to be euthanized. Cheryl and Manlio did not communicate that to me. Cheryl took her away from me and I was not ever able to say goodbye to my best friend at the time. I never think about this by the way. This is probably the first time in 25 years that I have thought about this.

Where's Penne? I said in a panic to Cheryl when she came home.

Penne developed doggy diabetes and so Penne is now in doggy heaven.

If I were any other little boy or girl I would have immediately started to cry. I would have immediately run to my "mother's" arms to be consoled. As I'm thinking about this right now, I can't help but wonder if that was her fucked up plan all along. Because of everything you've read so far, I was not a very affectionate boy with either of my parents. And when Cheryl announced that Penne was no more, I calloused my mind.

Your brother has diabetes. And it is treatable.

That costs money. And you know what that requires right?

Of course. Monitoring of blood glucose levels, a specific diet, and insulin injections.

That's expensive Gavi! Aren't you even going to show that you care about her?

Are you fucking kidding me you fucking asshole, is the thought that I had.

Why didn't you tell me that this was happening today? I had offered that I wanted to go.

We thought it would be better for you this way.

And that was the end of the dialogue because I turned around, went to my room which was my only sanctuary and closed the door. *Better for me this way.* I want you to know Dear Reader, that today, finally today, as I write these words, I am finally grieving the loss of my first dog Penne. As a pet owner today, with another one of the sweetest little girls on the planet, who is now an elderly doggy, DoYoung and I are anxious about the day when our daughter's faculties start to fail. We cry every time it happens to come up. We've seen a bit of decline in her hind legs and have

198

made a bucket list of items for our little Tupal to complete so that we know we have given her the best life possible.

Anyway…Fuck you Cheryl! I don't think I will ever be able to forgive you for not giving me an opportunity to let Penne know how much I loved her, to hold her in a warm embrace one last time, to rub her little belly, to scratch behind her little ears, and to say my apologies for ever treating her badly, to let her know that "she was just the best girl ever" and to say my goodbyes. I loved Penne so much. Other than my grandma, my dad, and my cousins, I loved nothing else except for Penne. She was always there for me. I actually right now am having some memories of how I would have long conversations with her. She would listen very intently and cock her head to the side when something struck her as curious. We were inseparable. She would often be in my bed after an episode with Cheryl and we would snuggle together through the night and keep each other warm. It was the only consolation in my childhood. And on top of that, I don't even have one picture of her that I can glance at on occasion. Penne, you were the best little doggy for me. You and grandma, I think the both of you, are the reasons I am who I am today. I will think of you more because I want you to still exist with me.

My dad did not travel very often for work and when he did Cheryl's impact on me would worsen. She had this fixation and fantasy that eventually I would agree to being adopted by her so that instead of her being my stepmom she would actually be my mom. Does this even make any fucking sense? Honestly, I believe she was obsessed with this idea to the point that it influenced all of her interactions with me. Thanks to Cheryl and her molesting of me I would later come to find out that I had intimacy issues. No, I was not impotent and have never been. However, actually initiating intimacy was a problem. When you have a step mother who is out to literally fuck you while also brainwashing you into believing that if I were to have sex with anyone other than someone that I was married to that "you'll burn ever after in the fiery pits of hell you god damned sonofabitch".

One time my dad went on a business trip to Argentina. He was gone for an eternity as far as I was concerned. Due to finances or probably to get away from *her* stupid ass, he went by himself and left Cheryl to parent me alone. By now, I had grown a little smarter about how to counteract Cheryl's visits. For one thing, I had learned how to pretend sleep. I would intentionally stay awake and listen for her approach, her footsteps. When I picked up her approach I would breath deeply and rhythmically as though I were asleep. Cheryl would approach my bedroom door gingerly, open it as quietly as she possibly could, and stand in the doorway for many minutes observing and evaluating if I were asleep or not. If she determined that I was asleep most times she would remain uninterested and quietly close the door and retreat to her room. If she determined I was awake, then I was in for a long night of defending myself.

One night, while my dad was probably living his best life in Argentina, Cheryl did not care if I was asleep or not. She burst through the door and shook me so that I had no choice except to be awake. Penne ran out of the room perhaps fleeing for her life. *Take me with you* was a thought that occurred to me. Cheryl climbed into the bed and turned me to one side so that she could spoon me. She was sobbing uncontrollably while also wet kissing me everywhere on my neck and bare back. Sobbing turned into erotic breathing. And her hands were everywhere on me. Rubbing my chest. Rubbing my thighs. And she did in fact move her hands to my groin. She also placed herself on me and was dry humping me from behind. I was paralyzed. Frozen in fear. My dad wasn't here. It would always be her word against mine. Then her hands moved to my hands and she made a very strong attempt to make me finger her. And that's when I finally woke up!

Stop it! You fucking stop it right now!

I was livid, is an understatement. I became rage.

I was an elite athlete as a punk ass. 3% body fat and also I could lift double my weight in all major muscle groups. I played soccer, baseball, tennis, golf, football, wrestling, and I ran track too. I jumped out of bed. She did too. I punched her as hard as I could in the stomach. And then, I did not know I had such strength, but I picked her up and literally threw her down the hallway. To the gut punch she had doubled over and was struggling to catch her breath as I knocked it right out of her. The shock on her face from being thrown down the hall actually amused me a little and I couldn't help myself, I started to laugh uncontrollably. I had tears in my eyes I was laughing so hard. When it passed I stared her down attempting to predict what might happen next. She remained there, on the ground, startled.

I was still rage.

If you ever put your fucking hands on me again, I will fucking kill you. You are not allowed to touch me. Not even a fucking hand shake.

I meant it too. I would fucking kill her. She had gathered herself by now. She stood up. And without any warning or any sign of what was going to happen next she bull rushed me. I process information at an incredibly high speed. I've come to learn in recent years that I have immediate replay and that by the time something is about to conclude, that I've already replayed it in triplicate so that when it actually concludes I have already lined up a number of options to consider and then actually I am already ready to act on one of those options. In this episode, I used her own momentum against her and when she was close enough to me I was able to launch her again and so I launched her into a wall. I had thrown her so hard using her momentum that the plaster caved in and left a huge hole in the wall. My hope was that we finally had a catalyst, evidence that I could use to finally let my dad know what had been going on. That hope was short lived as her brother arrived the next day to fix and paint the wall. She made up some story, you know, some kind of trip and fall accident. Just like that, the evidence was eliminated and as I've already stated it would be her word against mine. This was how I thought about it anyway.

We did have one more physical alteration after that. I won that one too. All I will say about that one was that she had actually made an attempt to choke me. She had her man hands around my neck and attempted to take my life. I quite violently threw her to the ground and that was the end of that attempt.

I was fury this time. I snarled at her.

You are a fucking waste of oxygen. You are fucking weak in all aspects. You can't hurt me in any regard. Fuck off.

I walked away and she never made any other attempt to try and touch me sexually after that. At least not privately. Years later when DoYoung and I had just started dating, Cheryl tried to establish some kind of female dominance to let DoYoung know that she was the first woman to make contact with my groin. The four of us, my dad, Cheryl, DoYoung and I were at a shooting range. We were shooting clay pigeons. I was using my great grandpa's 12 gauge. And Cheryl had picked it up for me. She walked over to DoYoung and I where we were busy flirting in between shots. Cheryl stands right in front of us, is holding the shotgun out towards me, looks me in the eye and with her man voice has the fucking nerve to say, "You know what you need to do". In case I'm not being clear here, what Cheryl meant by that, was than in order for her to handover the shotgun to me, that she was expecting that I would kiss her. Yep! What the actual fuck! "No. Give me the gun". Her pea brain actually had to think about it. She was about to open her mouth to say some dumb fucking comment and then decided otherwise and handed me the gun. "Thank you!" (Asshole!). DoYoung said, "what was that?". I'll tell you later was my reply. And I did tell her later. I told her about all of the things you've read so far, Dear Reader.

Chapter 13

We were a median income family especially with only one working parent. That said, money by no stretch of the imagination was tight. Well, I mean it was tight because my parents were religious and tithed the amount that the Bible dictates. Also, I went to private school. It was costly. I'm not a subscriber. That's not a judgment on my part if you are a subscriber please do not be offended. My point is that they could have saved those dollars. And of course there were the payments made for the health of my biological mother. My parents had a very strict outlook on life and also a paranoid one. My dad would often go on the record and say, "everyone is out to get your money, Gavi, and don't you forget it". I never took him seriously on that advice and I should have because when he meant everyone, I think he also meant himself and Cheryl. Definitely fucking Cheryl.

Cheryl complained about money every day and mostly how I cost them so much. You know, with my need for clothes, food, and school supplies etc. You know, the basics and fundamentally what is required of parents to provide for their children. She was always in my ear about how much I cost them with Yvonne's medical bills. I worked really hard in school and I had straight As. I also worked really hard at home. I cut the grass. I did the dishes. I did my own laundry. I read books. I watched a little TV too. But mostly, I was really autonomous and kept to myself in my bedroom with my over active imagination. Also, I was not paid an allowance like most kids. In the summers where I was not visiting my grandparents, I started a little business so that I could make some money to buy some comic books and other items that were not allowed to be purchased with my dad's hard earned money.

One day while riding my bike through the neighborhood I observed that someone had thrown away a lawn mower. It was just sitting there next to the trash receptacles. And it was obvious that it was being thrown away because it was sitting on top of the trash bags. Little Gavi had the instant idea of starting a lawn cutting business. I dragged the lawn mower behind me as I rode home and my mind was racing at how to bring this idea to life. I was very motivated. I took the lawn mower to behind our garage. No one can see behind the garage and for obvious reasons I wanted all of this to be private. I do actually remember being anxious about any random insults that would be thrown at me by *her*.

So, on a hot summer day, I proceeded to examine the root cause on why the lawn mower was discarded. I should mention that I did try to get the mower to start. It had gas. It had oil. It would not crank over. I had no idea what I was doing and to this day I can tell you that I am not mechanically inclined. I grabbed all the tools I thought I would need and I took the lawn mower engine apart piece by piece cataloguing in my mind the order of the disassembly so that when I felt I had fixed the machine it would easily be reassembled. I had purpose. I had intent and I was highly motivated.

Several hours later, I had just completely reassembled the machine and I heard my dad come home. He had just parked his car in the garage and he heard me banging around. He came to the back of the garage and with a puzzled look on his face, "what are you doing there Gavi?". I explained my plan to him and to my surprise he was actually open to the idea and was going to support me on this. And then something magical happened. I had not yet attempted after the reassembly to try to get it to run.

Watch this dad!

I pulled the rope and on the first crank the engine turned over and I had successfully resurrected this lawn mower! My dad stood there bewildered and his eyes were wide.

Dad, I need to borrow some money. I think about $50. I'll pay you back. Mom is always complaining to me that the money is super tight and I don't want anyone to be in trouble. The fifty bucks will be used for gasoline, oil, I need a new blade, and well, I'm going to make a trailer so that I can put all my supplies on it and tow it behind my bike. I'm going to go door to door in the neighborhood and where I can see that people need their grass cut, I'm going to knock on their door and I'm going to ask for $15 bucks a lawn. I need a weed wacker and an edger too. And extension cords for the weed whacker.

Tell you what Gavi. I have no idea what your mother is talking about. Our finances are perfect so don't you worry about that. Use our weed wacker and use our extensions cords. As far as the materials for the trailer, they're on me. It looks like I should give you some advice on finances and what it means to save money Gavi, so let's do that tonight. I'll cover the new blade too. I have no idea where this lawn mower came from or how you fixed it. But as I live and breathe there it is and you did that. I'm proud of you son. Oh, you need safety goggles and safety boots.

That summer I made a $1000 in profits. I think I was not more than twelve and definitely not more than fourteen.

I had a lot of fun making that $1000. Think about that, it's a lot of lawns. Well, there were some tips. I learned a lot about myself that summer. I learned that stay at home mothers, for example, were my number one demographic. I had a number of lawns that would become routine. The same day of the week. The same friendly faces of stay at home mothers. I found many of them to be very nice and sweet. As it was the middle of the summer, and in Michigan, hot and humid, I often found myself shirtless. Cutting, edging, weed whacking, riding a bike and towing all of my equipment behind me had me quite lean and muscular. Also, I reached puberty earlier than most boys and I as I said previously became "aware". Aware that these beautiful moms would come out and chat with me. They would "check in" with me, bring me water, kool aid, lemonades, and you know run their fingers through my air or bring me a fresh, cool towel and waited and watched as I drank or toweled off.

Of course being a polite, young boy ("Always be a gentleman") and also because I loved talking with nice, and beautiful women, I would always engage. I've been told I have WOO (Winning Others Over) and that I can be a very charming person. I promise I had worthy intent. I was not out to break up any marriages, for example. But because I was this polite, apparently good looking, muscular force, who was also doing something nice for them, something unexpected happened. (And Dear Reader, I know you can see where this is going).

It was an afternoon and Leslie's Lawn was on the schedule. Leslie was a tall, slender, blue-eyed, big bosomed blonde bomb shell. She had a warm and inviting smile, eyes that twinkled like stars. Her long hair was always meticulous and her nails were always manicured, painted, and flawless. She wore diamond everything, especially her wedding rings. That afternoon, Leslie came out to meet me as she normally would and she engaged in a conversation that I will never forget.

Her voice sounding sultry…

Gavi, how old are you? Be honest with me now. It matters.

I'm 15 Leslie.

That was a lie. As I just mentioned I was maybe 12 and definitely not more than 14.

Are you sure you're not 16, Gavi (followed by a little "hmm" and a slight touch on the wrist)

Now, in grade school, I had lots of friends who are also girls. I had lots of friends and I loved talking to the prettiest girls in the room. They in turn loved talking to me and so I learned early on that I might actually be a good looking dude (but that I was "always to be a gentleman" and that I also was probably "going to hell if I ever acted on my feelings towards these girls). And as such, it all stayed platonic (as it should in gradeschool / first years of high school). Anyway, with Leslie, and what was happening, I felt my heart pounding in my chest and also this warm, fuzzy feeling came over. It was intoxicating. I found myself staring into her eyes and also this new feeling, which as an adult I now know as desire.

I'll just be direct now: And my dick got hard! (which I in my short lawn cutting shorts, I could not hide).

This is where it obviously could have gone horribly wrong. Leslie, I guess, I was surprised and impressed at the same time and thank the stars she treated me delicately, especially with what you know as you keep getting through these pages, Dear Reader.

Leslie placed her sweet, soft hand into mine, and whispered in my ear, "It's ok Gavi. I've got you. Come with me". And for the sake of this book not completely being about sexual experiences, both good and horrid, I will just say that that summer was the most erotic year of my life and I learned everything in that summer that would carry me forward with girlfriends, fiancés, and my wife. (sorry DoYoung). I found myself wishing that the grass would grow faster. Of course when a boy is no longer a boy, it is distinctly observable. Hygiene and shaving become a priority. Hell, just maintaining a hair style suddenly is a priority. Leslie noticed these changes and complimented me and it made the summer even that much more enjoyable (both for her and me). Cheryl also noticed these changes. As dumb as she was did start noticing that there was particular day of the week where I would be "different".

Cheryl followed me one day as I made my way to Leslie's. As was our routine, I still had to take care of the lawn and when I was about to finish, Leslie would come outside, offer me a water, take my hand, and walk me inside where we would start with a shower etc…If Leslie did not come out then that was our signal that Mr. Leslie might be home and that she might otherwise be obligated. Leslie had always kept up appearances and so she never dressed provocatively to bring me inside, still by comparison to Cheryl, Leslie was opposite in all ways. And since Cheryl was trying to fuck me and Leslie actually was, Cheryl was rage! Well, what I mean to say is that she became enraged later. When I got home…

Where were you today and don't you fucking lie to me because I already know the fucking truth! You're a fornicator! You're going to rot in hell you shit!

By this time, I was over it. I was over *her*. Afterall, I had this amazing older, beautiful woman who was sweet to me, treated me well, was kind, thoughtful, and well, sorry, satisfied my baser desires (even if you're thinking it's wrong, Dear Reader and well, I don't care what you think about that because I actually had something nice in my life for a change). I very calmy said...

I wonder what place your god has in store for you based on your treatment of me. I have been fornicating. And I love it!

And then I smiled. A big, ear to ear shit eating grin. She bull rushed me. That was my plan as soon as I realized I was being confronted. Also, you think she would have learned by now that this was not going to work out the way she had imagined.

I brought her to the ground, and choked her out until she passed out. She came to about the same time my dad came home from work but still had enough time to recover and hide any evidence of our altercation. Then she surprised me. I could not have predicted this. She told on me! (are you fucking kidding me?!)

Manlio! Your son has been having sex with a married woman down the street. He has sex after he cuts the lawn.

It must have been the innuendoes lawn cutting reference. You know, like, yeah, I sure did cut that lawn! Because my dad burst out into uncontrollable laughter. I was never confronted by my dad about this and instead, just like that, all of my lawn cutting equipment was dismantled and discarded. I obviously was no longer going to be able to take care of lawns. Additionally, Cheryl took all of my money that I had earned. Poof. I sometimes wonder if Leslie ever thought of what happened to me. Nah, she was probably very grateful that I just stopped showing up. I hope she felt like it was a wonderful experience. Leslie, if you ever read this book and you realize it's you in this story, then all I can say is that you came into my life when it was shit, and you showed me that not all women are trying to fuck their own sons or abuse them. Also, I think you made me realize that sex, when reciprocated, is fucking healthy! Thank you for that Leslie (it certainly saves my therapist some time there although I think she would disagree and would try to make me realize that this too is not normal or natural and should not have happened because this woman also took advantage of you – I know!).

We have a plan for our life Gavi. You fucking ruin it every day. Every time your glasses break it costs us money. All this food

I make is not free don't cha know! You come home from school and you have stains and holes in your clothes. You have no respect for how hard your father works.

Actually I have no respect for your methods. If I had contacts, for example, my glasses wouldn't break…(deep sigh…)

Chapter 14

At just barely 18 years old and two weeks after graduating high school I was in the Army in Basic Training. Dear Reader, at the risk of boring you to death with disgusting story after disgusting story, I will simply highlight two more and I promise that in the next chapter we'll move on to the brighter side. After all this is a tale of three mothers! And believe me, I have not touched the tip of the iceberg with other very horrific tales.

I exited the military after four years and exited as a Sergeant. I had made Sergeant in 2 years and 10 months which is fast especially during times of peace. I exited to pursue a Bachelor of Science at Eastern Michigan University. In order to prepare for that exit, I had to travel from Frederick, MD to Ypsilanti, MI to lease an apartment, order text books and etc. Well, I called my dad up to see if I could stay at their house while I was going to be in Michigan for perhaps three days in order to make all of the necessary arrangements. To my surprise, he said "no". (*Asshole!*) I never did get an explanation for that. So, I was not smart enough at the time to think of booking a hotel room. In fact, I was not experienced in life yet to know that hotel rooms were even an option. So, in one day, I drove from Frederick, MD to Ypsilanti, MI, bought all of my text books, met with school counselors, paid my college tuition for the upcoming semester, secured an apartment, and drove back to Frederick, MD. You read that correctly. The universe really helped me out there by aligning all of the things all at once so that I could be a ridiculous human being and drive to and from MI to MD in the same damn day. Dear Dad, you're a fucking asshole and you're weak!

In two and a half years I completed my Bachelor of Science degree. I was also working full time and upon graduating, the company I worked for promoted me and relocated me to Stockton, CA. The next set of details about the story are for a different volume Dear Reader, but I will say that I was not ready to be in the fast paced life of California. I had a mental and nervous breakdown and after 6 months I tendered my resignation. I literally quit my job without having another job lined up and I packed up all of my shit and moved back into my parents house in Michigan. I'm in my mid-twenties if you're still keeping up with the chronology of events.

While I was living there, and I should mention I had no money, Cheryl convinced Manlio that I was to pay for rent, food, utilities, phone, cable, so on and so forth. Cool, thanks so much for hitting me below the belt while I was already down for the count. Of course she pedantically suggested that I could go be a greeter at Walmart. (Fuck you!). In short order, I was able to be in touch with my former network in the military and I quickly found a job back in the pharmaceutical world and swiftly moved out and moved to North Carolina. To be clear, I moved from Michigan to California, California to Michigan, and Michigan to North Carolina in the stretch of 6 months. Stressful! Anyway, here's the point of this story: A month later I received a letter in the mail from Cheryl informing me that I needed to pay for $15 of their phone bill. My use of the phone from Michigan to my new place of employ had raised their bill by $15 and *she* could not let that go. Give me a fucking break.

The other thing worth mentioning is that my Dad really did me a nice favor once. He took out a second mortgage on the house so that I could fund the rest of my tuition for undergrad. I agreed to their terms of paying it back each month. Then at the same time I moved to North Carolina, Cheryl announced to me that I would have to pay the 2nd mortgage off three years ahead of the mortgage schedule. It was a directive. It was not a request.

Dear Reader, these details matter for this next chapter so just bear with me a little longer.

I often ask myself, Gavi, how are you not a psychopath serial killer? To summarize, I had two women figures in my life who wanted to fuck me, who spoke vulgarities to me, and made me handle them, and also they actually handled me. But, to not an extent of intercourse. I was robbed of my childhood by these women, I had a dad who didn't step in, and at this point, I still felt obligated to maintain the relationship. I also was actually robbed. Every dollar I had ever made while working at a golf course, at Ponderosa, and my little lawn cutting business, was put into their bank accounts for their purposes. They probably needed a little extra to tithe or you know, I was probably paying for my own groceries.

Later, in the military, while talking to my best bud, I learned that I was supposed to be in charge of my money that I was earning for doing my job. I was not in charge of my checkbook, Cheryl was. She thought she was doing me a favor by managing my money for me. "Managing". More like pilfering. So after two years in the military, I still had no money saved and then they had the nerve to say they paid for my college. Say what??!!

The stupidity goes on and on. I hope I've painted a clear picture.

Chapter 15

Some several years ago my biological grandfather passed away. To the day, exactly one year later, my biological mother died. To the day, exactly one year after that one year, my grandmother exited the planet The first two losses…eh, they were losses.

Grandma leaving the planet had a devastatingly profound impact on me, that I still emote over even after several years. Her passing also began the point in time where I was disowned by my biological father, and I realized, I would no longer label his wife anything other than, "your wife". Read this very clearly: Adult Gavi was no longer going to call that woman, "mom".

It has been five years since any of us have picked up the phone or emailed, or been in touch.

I've always only expected one thing from DoYoung when she has to be around my family. Please just say "hello [insert person's name]", and complete an obligatory hug, while politely smiling. That's it. And that's because for some weird reason, anything less than that or even more than that results in a shitshow of poor behaviors from family members. The stories here are too numerous to count and also pointless to put in print.

This day was not going to be an exception.

DoYoung performed her obligation with Cheryl. Immediately Cheryl points at DoYoung, and with a growling snarl, says, "That's It?!!". DoYoung calmy replied back, "what more are you looking for?". And then, rightly so walked away. I saw and heard the whole thing. Yet Cheryl immediately went to Manlio to complain how DoYoung had just insulted her by calling her some inflammatory name and that also she didn't get the hug she was expecting, which was some insane made-up lie. In the Bizarro universe Cheryl also expects that their relationship will be like Mother / Daughter. Um, excuse me, DoYoung already has a mom.

That's point 1 of what would become the prospective disowning.

Anyway, later in the day, Cheryl wants us to all take pictures. Now, we had all just taken pictures at my grandfather's funeral and for me personally, I did not think it was a great way to honor him. I certainly was not going to entertain photos for Grandma's funeral. We announced this ahead of the event even. That we're not comfortable with taking photos on the day of Grandma's funeral. Afterall, as close as I was to grandma, I did not see myself wanting to pose and smile for *Cheryl's* edification.

Cheryl proceeded to order all who were there to line up for photos. We said, "No". We encouraged others to say "No". And before you knew it, everyone was saying "No". Enter point 2 on why we were disowned.

I have a California family now and so I say good riddance! You all are moronic red-neck trailer trash anyway and it's not like we have anything in common.

A few months later, I received a call from my dad because "he had a bone to pick with me".

You were really disrespectful at grandma's funeral Gavi. You did our family name a disservice. You need to apologize to me and your mother. And what the fuck did your asshole of a wife say to Cheryl? I've been dealing it with ever since!

Well dad, actually I found it really disrespectful that Cheryl wanted to take pictures. I did not find that to be a favorable way to honor Grandma at her funeral. And by the way, I saw and heard the whole interaction between Cheryl and DoYoung and DoYoung is in the right and your asshole of a wife is lying to you, like she has all of your marriage. Also, if anyone is doing a disservice to the Donato namesake, it's your asshole of a wife. And I'll just go ahead and say it, both of you are assholes and are very deserving of each other. We are adults over here after all and you'll fucking recognize it. You'll fucking recognize that I don't have to follow your instructions and I certainly don't need you in my life to validate my existence or my success.

You'll watch your tone with me. I brought you into this life and I'll take you out of this life.

Good luck with that. You might also want to watch how you threaten me; I'm married to a lawyer. And since this a phone conversation, I would love for you to say something to me like that in person. You're a weak man who's forgotten how to use his brain, and you'd be lucky to take out a snail.

There was silence on both ends of the line for a while. And then...

Hey, I hate your wife, I and think she's the spawn of Satan.

Hey, I love my wife, so FUCK OFF! And let's be clear on what you hate. You hate that she's smarter than you, has ambition, is articulate, intelligent, and gorgeous. In other words, all of the things that you're unable to tolerate or accept as an old, insecure white man. I mean, how dare she have an education and a position in conversations! Grow up! Don't let the door hit you, where the good Lord split you!

Click. Bring in the sound of the dial tone.

At Grandma's funeral there were two members of the audience who eulogized her. My Dad. Me.

My Dad went first. He pulled out a three-ring binder. And very matter of fact did his best David Copperfield. She was born. he grew into an adult and had these professions. She died. From my perspective, it was completely devoid of emotion and the eulogy lacked substance. Weak.

He ended the eulogy by asking if anyone else would like to say a few words. I hate to admit this but I grew nervous and I almost could not pull myself together. DoYoung put her hand on my shoulder, "You got this". And so I did and I announced that I would like to say a few words. Interestingly, I saw that that made my dad a twitch nervous.

Good afternoon. It's nice to see you all today; you all look lovely.

As I look around the room, I think I know most everyone here, but just in case we've never met before:

I'm Gavi Donato. I traveled here from Thousand Oaks, CA with my beautiful wife, DoYoung, to honor Carmen. I'm the son of Manlio, which makes me a grandson, of Carmen.

Today, I offer you a few words from the perspective of a grandson.

I think, for several of us in the room (cousins), we had a different way of life to start our lives for 1) an extended period of time that was particularly tumultuous for our parents, and 2) deliberately with what ends up being probably the most amazing summer camps, in the U.P. (yah, don't ya know).

In case it's not clear, I just told you that we spent many years with Grandma and Grandpa, in essence, being raised by them as if we were their own kids.

Grandma would later tell our mothers: "Those are my kids; they're mine now".

And it was true. And it wasn't an insult to our mothers; I believe it was pride that Grandma had inside of her for raising us. I also think it was Grandma's way of saying that she felt an intense sense of ownership for who we were at that moment in time; and then ultimately who we would become as functioning adults in society primarily as a result of her tutelage.

For me, that's critical, because there is absolutely a line of demarcation in who I probably was going to be without Grandma

225

in my early life, versus who I actually became because of Grandma's involvement. It.Is.Absolutely.Undeniable!

As many of you know, here in the later years, Grandma suffered from dementia and she lost us in the same way we lost her. I think she got the benefit of that in that equation. She was happy and sweet without too much of a care in the world while we were the ones suffering the loss of the amazing individual who was also so intricately involved in all aspects of our life.

With that in mind, I actually have had over 5 years to be introspective about life lessons that Grandma taught us; that means, quite literally, in a final lucid moment between Grandma and I, we each, in our own way, said goodbye to each other.

So, I am deeply hurt by the loss of the physical entity that was our Grandma; that was our mom, but her voice is in my head as part of a trio of people who make up my conscience. She's in there still telling me, still guiding me on "right and wrong". By the way, there's a psychological term for that; it's called your "inner speech".

The introspective look I just mentioned gave me a "top" list of Grandma's lessons for a happy and healthy life. Some of these may sound a bit cliché but hang with me because I've got an amazing surprise for you.

Ok, Grandma's Lessons:

1. Be Nice to People

a. Did you know that on Earth, over time, there have been 6 species of humans, and that, we, the current and only species, Homo Sapiens, wiped out all the other species. Why am I telling you this: We're all cut genetically from the same genes. Our blood is red.

b. Grandma taught us early to be nice to people; life is one large lesson in managing perception, and where you might not need help now, you might at some point, and if you're a big meany, you will probably be alone and without the help you need, when you do need it.

I started with that lesson and looked directly at Cheryl the whole time. She grew visibly uncomfortable.

2. Pinch Your Pennies

a. Grandma taught us the value of saving money. She taught us that, money, as a resource was powerful but limited.

b. And although she told us to pinch our pennies, I think, on a daily basis, she was also out there earning her own pennies and absolutely winning more and more pennies at bingo and the slots at the casino.

3. Spank Your Kids

227

a. As her kids we had an unexpected freedom to explore our individuality. She let us roam, explore, learn, and fend for ourselves. And in so doing, we were not controlled and we were able to begin to understand who we were and what we were interested in.

b. And when we crossed a line, which we often did, we felt the full wrath of her discipline.

c. In getting ready for this eulogy the cousins and I recalled a fond memory. I broke a plastic rifle over my female cousin by clubbing her with it. In turn, Grandma broke all of her wooden cooking spoons over my hinny.

4. Chivalry

a. It sounds weird right now, but chivalry is mostly dead. I'm not going to go into detail on why, but I could.

b. I had a girlfriend in the UP during those summers. When Grandma learned of that, instead of telling me I was going to hell for it, she took the time to teach me chivalry. "Open the door for her, Mike" and other such chivalrous guidelines that I still follow today. DoYoung is very appreciative of those life lessons.

5. Keep Your Head Up

a. She would not want us to be sad for her today.

b. She would be happy that we are all together today, to remember her, to honor her.

c. She would tell us to keep our head up and when life is getting us down to "keep smiling, baby!"

d. "Keep smiling", which would immediately be followed up by a drag on a filtered cigarette, a sip of coffee or wine, depending on the time of day, and that wonderful "ha-ha" chuckle that we all love so well.

On facebook last week, I wrote about how we all used to watch MTV with Grandma.

As I was writing this in the lobby of the hotel this morning, and I'm pretty sure Grandma was with me, because no joke, in succession, Def Leppard, Guns 'N' Roses, Poison, Michael Jackson, Rod Steward, and George Michael played. These obviously are artists we would watch in the late eighties on MTV together where Grandma would get up and dance with us. She'd also ask who all of these pretty women were when we watched Poison. And for at least two people in the room, the Cookie Monster song came on...

Finally: I offer these words that come directly from Grandma and is absolutely fitting.

Cousin Ricardo found this yesterday while we were looking through photos and I'm pretty sure Grandma reached out and placed it right into his hands for this very moment. We offer you

this poem written by Grandma. And without giving too much away,
I think you'll appreciate Grandma's sense of humor and irony.

With that: "Michigan, My Michigan"

It's winter here in Michigan and the gentle breeze blow 70 miles

Per hour;
At 22 below, Oh, how I love my Michigan.
When the snow's up to my butt,
I take a breath of winter air, and freeze my nostrils shut.
Yes, the weather here is wonderful,
So, I guess I'll hang around,
I could never leave Michigan,

I'm frozen to the ground.

Grandma's final life lesson: Don't take yourself so seriously.

Thank you.

There wasn't a dry eye in the house. DoYoung rushed up to me and embraced me for a long time.

I learned much later from DoYoung that pretty much Grandma was the only family member who told her that she loved her and that she loved how happy I was being with her. DoYoung also holds a special place in her heart for Carmen and we talk about it often in remembrance of her and to keep her an active part of our life.

Other audience members, like Ricardo, my brother, also came up to give me a hug. Ricardo was quick to compliment me, "That's the way you do it brother". What he meant was, I took everyone in the room on a journey to remember her, to feel her, to conjure her to our mind's eye and that's the god damned point of a eulogy, thank you very much.

Even right now, many years later after her lucid death and her corporeal death and I still cannot get past the line, "I could never leave Michigan". I get that lump in the throat and the tears arrive. I miss her everyday. In that moment when we said goodbye to each other, she handed me a quilt that she had just completed. To keep her with me everyday, I have that quilt displayed on my man-cave couch. When I watch TV by myself I like to think she's there with me getting ready to get up and dance, or just relax with a sip of wine.

Because I think of her often, she is still here. I cannot say I still hear her guiding my conscience and a close friend and psychologist told me that it is actually a good thing. I do not need the guiding voice. I'm my own North Star now.

Grandma was my North Star for 35 years of my life. I feel fortunate to have had such tremendous force for good in my life. Because as a young kid, and after experiencing violence and abuse, and at about the time I was attempting to murder seagulls and other small animals, Grandma recognized my evil and course corrected me into the fine gentleman I am today.

Another one of her life lessons was that if you do not go and get your education, then you'll be digging ditches for a living. And when Ricardo found himself digging ditches, he said, "well shit, grandma was right, I'm going to school imminently". (and he did too!)

Grandma cultivated me into the fine man I am today. I want you to know Dear Reader, that none of the atrocities I faced growing up have defined me. I became Antifragile. I became an evolved human who developed superpowers. Life is a battlefield and in the trenches I keep coming out on top. I live a life of the charmed with a successful career, amazing life-long friends (family), and a beautiful immediate family with now two French Bulldogs. My disposition is loving, caring, and thoughtful of those around me. I have only Grandma to thank for who I became and who I am today. She introduced me to the wide, vast world while others tried to contain and subdue me to their narrowminded perspectives. She gave me a chance to have a different view of the world because afterall, she too was not of this world.

DoYoung is what I like to call an Alpha-Female. Grandma, ahead of her time, was also an Alpha-Female. In fact, I surround myself with Alpha-Females because I can not tolerate anything less than. Actually, I extricate anything less than. DoYoung and I had considered eloping and it was my persistence in wanting to have Grandma see us get married that we agreed to hold a wedding event.

We kept it small. Although Cheryl tried to take over the event but we had planned family members to run interference. In fact, I even had the DJ involved to help with interference. DoYoung and I had both secretly agreed that there could not be a Daughter / Daddy dance and there would definitely not be a Cheryl / Gavi dance. However, we did swing a Gavi / Grandma dance.

Grandma was dressed pretty in a pink dress. She was full of life. She likes to tell everyone that she was 18 years young. She had brought her traditional Italian wedding cookies. Grandma was superstitious and while we danced she told me how DoYoung and I both needed to eat the cookies simultaneously to bring us good luck and vibrant health.

Grandma imparted these words to me while we were dancing and please read this in a thick Italian accent:

Gavi, I love you. You've always been my favorite son, but shh, don't tell anyone, ha-ha.

You're the only one who listened to me and you and Ricardo are the only one whose made something of themselves.

Good for you! I'm proud of you. You're very successful, you're using that big brain, and when I predict the future for you, everything turns out exactly as it should. Trust me, all good things.

Your wife is beautiful! I love her.

And if you love her, you go early and you love her! Ha-ha.

Don't you worry about what your asshole of a stepmother says or does. She's a fucking idiot! Pardon my French.

You're dad married idiots twice! And shame on him.

Always make your wife your top priority Gavi, and everything else will fall into place.

She makes you a better you, and I want you to know that I see that.

The two of you are going to have a wonderful life together. It will be hard. Just remember all I taught you.

I did not want the song to end.

I'm not always going to be here for you. I will always be with you, right here.

She put her hand on my heart. Then she put both of her hands on my face, held them there in soft motherly caress, kissed my left cheek, kissed my right cheek, and then the song ended.

Thank you Grandma, thank you mom, I mean, I love you.

THE END

Epilogue

Dear Reader, it took me a decade to write Volume 1. Not consecutively of course. It wasn't until DoYoung and I separated, where I went into therapy and realized what I went through was not normal. We separated because I became "excessive" and was commonly in a downward spiral. We're still together and thriving. For me, going through this, I just thought this was normal, a rite of passage into adulthood. Obviously, I now know differently. All of that said, it still does not define me.

This volume starts off with how this will be an evaluation leading to a decision of having kids or not having kids. DoYoung and I have kids, the fur baby kind. And we love our life that way. We've also witnessed first hand how kids (1 can be an absolute blessing for a couple or 2) how it can be absolute nightmare where our closest friends have divorced. We believe that with our ambitious careers that we would fall into category 2 and we're fine just the way we are with our freedom, and our Frenchies. Although, we would make one hell of an amazing kid.

Could we love kids in our life?

Absolutely.

Our friends have enough children for both of us to live vicariously through them.

Finally, I wonder if any of you have put any thought into why this is titled the "The Revisionist".

You might find this to be some kind of cruel joke to now reveal that this is just a story. It could be my story. It could be a true story. It could be that I completely made this up. I challenge you to determine what you think is real versus what is made up. Afterall, I am The Revisionist. And after all Dear Reader, you made the choice to take this on.

And I thank you.

Appendix 1 – An Exercise in Therapy
Think about the Chair – What's in the Chair (13SEP2023)

At first, I felt horrified to "think about the chair".

When thinking about this innocuous object, it was as if a dark shadow suddenly enveloped me.

Nothing else really exists in that moment except that dark shadow when the therapist pulls out the chair, and says, "think about the chair, Gavi".

With the shadow there become an inability to breathe. I'm not voluntarily holding my breath, and I'm not, in the moment, aware that I'm holding my breath. Then the tears come. I don't know why the tears come and I'm not generally aware of what I'm thinking when it happens. Perhaps I'm thinking that I need to escape from that dark place and inevitably I'm conscious again. I can breathe again. And then the moment passes.

I've been thinking about the chair for nearly a week now.

As I think about the chair now, and nearly a week later, that horrific feeling has nearly completely subsided.

I want my therapist to know that thinking about the chair has been quite a journey.

The first time I started to deeply think about the chair a host of images were conjured to my mind's eye.

The images occurred in this order:

1. Grandma
2. Biological Mother
3. Dad
4. Stepmother

Grandma has never been associated to any darkness in my life other than to be a participant to particularly violent events originating with the Biological Mother.

Regarding the Biological Mother, I've settled that business in a very long chapter of the book. And because I have a specific belief that for as long as you continue to think about someone who has passed, then they still exist with you. I don't need for this person to exist so I do not think about this or her.

Regarding my Dad, that's unfinished business so it makes sense that I saw him. I saw him exactly once and it was fleeting at best.

I saw the stepmother the most. I know I have unsettled feelings about *her*. There's this show that is on Fx called, What we do in the Shadows. It's about vampires. It's a comedy. We used to watch it but then it became too repetitive. Anyway, one of the vampires does not suck blood for sustenance. Instead he drains people of their energy. He's an energy vampire. I would liken Cheryl to an Energy Vampire. She has to be the center of attention even though she's borderline handicapped, socially awkward, has to act like a general in the sense of everything needs to go according to her will, and all conversations inevitably have to be about something she's interested in; something she has a memory of. The conversations become kindergarten, and literally DoYoung and I feel as though we are losing brain cells; becoming dumber by the microsecond. Once, DoYoung and I were in a normal conversation with each other, and Cheryl butted in and said, "Don't use the words like that around me". Words with three syllables was her meaning. Can't even make shit like that up.

On top of that, there was the targeted abuse plus the fact that I was robbed of my childhood and of a relationship with my dad.

All of that said, I realized today that's still not what's in the chair. As I have said to you therapist, I don't really think about that and I don't really care about it and I feel like because I don't think about it and because I don't care, that it doesn't really impact me in present reality. I know you disagree.

So, what's in the chair? Why do I have this disgusting sense of dread when thinking about the chair? So much so that for no reason I can think of in the moment, I have an emotional outburst. Literally session one: "Close your eyes". Extreme discomfort and emotional expression.

The aforementioned, I think, have to make an appearance in the chair to channel that dark shadow, to channel that dread so that I can see what's actually there. The thing that I can't face is sitting there. Little Gavi is sitting there. He's sitting there, and fucking staring at me like in some Stephen King novel just patiently waiting for me to let him know he's going turn out ok. In fact, he's going to be some kind of super hero or "evolved human" as a doctor of mine likes to say.

So, Little Gavi, the time is almost near. Soon, I'll be able to look at you in the face, and reveal to you that which we've both been waiting for. We'll both be better and I just need a little more time.

Appendix 2: Traveling Back in Time to Talk to Little Gavi

Gavi, this is going to sound impossible and as you have an affinity for science fiction, my hope is that you'll be open to this. I'm you. I'm a much older version of you. If I've traveled back in time to the correct date, then you're about to be pre-teen, and well, I'm closer to fifty than I am forty.

Although you don't really understand this yet, you have suffered through some horrendous situations. Your murder has been attempted nearly a dozen times. You've been sexually molested. You've been verbally molested. You've been handed dangerous implements in the hopes that you would damage yourself or others. You've been witness to violent events. You've been placed into positions to make decisions that would determine your fate. You became a terminator so as not to be terminated. You became more than your genetics. You heightened all of your senses to self defend from a variety of predators.

Little Gavi – I want you to know that you turn out to be an amazing human being. You are very successful in several meaningful careers of which the current career affords you many perks not available to average human beings. You have a modern family with a loving and ambitious wife and you both care for two of the sweetest fur babies on the planet.

Little Gavi – You made intentional decisions early that helped you become antifragile. Fine, I'll say it to you, to be a survivor although you do not ever subscribe to victim mentality. I'm proud of you for fighting back. I'm proud of you for not giving in to pressure put on you by disturbed adults. Disturbed figure heads who were supposed to nurture you and show you appropriate love and care. The physical acts of violence that you had to act on to save yourself were appropriate. I know it made you feel guilty and angry. Those feelings are valid and you don't have to live with them any longer. You are safe. The worst of it is behind you. You lived through the worst of it already. They can't harm you any more. They are actually dead, or they are dead to you.

Little Gavi – You became a terminator so as not to be terminated. I am proud of you. The worst of it is behind you. You are welcome to keep your super powers. However, you don't really need them anymore. You're safe. Think about that you are safe. I've got you now. I can look at you, and I can talk to you whenever you want. I'm so very sorry about what you (we) went through. I'm so very sorry sorry it took me a lifetime to recognize you and set you free. But I've got you now and you can finally be a child. It's ok to turn off the scanning. Turn it on when you want to use it. It's ok to relax at night and go to sleep. You have a lovely home and it's safe from predators. It's ok, Gavi. It's ok. I promise that it's ok.

Little Gavi – It wasn't your fault. You did not do anything to provoke the adults. Enjoy the rest of your life guilt free. You've earned it and you deserve it. I love you.

Appendix 3: A letter never sent…

Dear Dad –

I sent you a text October 2022. Here's what it said:

"I have been on a self-realization journey this year and I have a story based on medical fact to tell you. If you're willing to hear this story for 15-20 minutes, then I believe it will help us in our current situation. After the story, I will give you an option. Let me know a good time that works for you. Now that I'm back from the company world tour I have more time than previously to discuss. If you're up for that, then let's limit this call to not more than 30 minutes. Same conditions as previously agreed to where no wives are in ear shot or on speaker phone for this conversation"

You didn't text back and we have not spoken by phone in over five years; not since the subsequent Mother's Day after Grandma's death. Thank you so much for sending me a box of all of the items that were left in your house, including the gifts that I had given to Cheryl for other Mother's Day's holidays. I threw all of those things out immediately. Of course I knew it was a ploy to get a reaction out of me. Didn't work out like you thought it would.

The origin of all my perceived rebellion goes all the way back to your decision where you required me to call Cheryl, "mom". Then after, you actually encouraged me to consider being adopted by that woman.

Were you completely unaware of what I was going through? I have to wonder if that's why you can't text or call – Perhaps you can't face me because you are aware and it's just easier to know that I'm living my best life without the two of you in California.

I sent you that text because I still desired a relationship with you. However, if you ever read this, then you'll finally understand why your position of also me having a relationship with Cheryl is impossible. Besides, she mistreats DoYoung and I just don't understand how you can't see it that way. And, how can you possibly still have a marriage with that woman if you did know she was abusing me? How can you have one now? She'll of course deny it and you'll believe her over me.

In any regard, we're very successful out here living our lives to the fullest. You're missing out. I'm your only child. I understand that you have to keep up appearances with your life partner but how does that qualify us as not having a relationship? My therapist has suggested that I just show up on your door some day before you die and tell you what I need to tell you. You have a belief that I should be subordinate and compliant. Good luck with that. I have a belief that we're to have equal give and take for the relationship to work. (And I'm sure you're saying the same thing: Good luck with that).

Finally, I realize those early years with Yvonne were tumultuous. Thank you for keeping me safe as best as you could. Thank you for putting yourself in harms way to project Little Gavi with the wackadoos. Thank you for placing me in Grandma's care. It's because of that that I'm not a psycho-path serial killer and perhaps why I'm not in jail or a sanitorium myself.

Perhaps some day we can raise a glass as we used to and smoke a cigar and relive the good stories of my childhood around a campfire. If you're angry, imagine how I feel. Cheryl, I think would have to be dead before you and I could catch up again. I will be sorry for your loss when that happens. I think she'll live longer than both of us though with all of her hate for everything that is good.

Anyway, I originally thought I was going to write a letter that was much more provocative.

This is what came out instead. Have a great rest of your life.

Love, Gavi.

Appendix 4: A letter never sent...

Dear Cheryl –

I once asked my dad, "what do you see in Cheryl; why are you together?" He responded with, "She gives me what I need". He couldn't elaborate further on what it was exactly that was needed or how you provide it which I find remarkable. I've put a lot of thought into this over the years and after having been married 13 years to DoYoung and together for 15 years and I can be very explicit about what I need and what DoYoung needs. I'm already wondering if you understand my meaning. My meaning: I can tell you what I need. DoYoung can tell you what she needs from me. So, how come Manlio cannot express what he means when he says, what he needs? It's very telling.

Here's what he needs...

• A placeholder human being to stay at home, clean the house, cut the lawn, iron his shirts, cook his meals, serve him a drink, and tend to his every whim. He could pay for these services and instead he married you to be subservient and because he knew he could control you.

• A placeholder human being to lie down in the missionary position to fill you up, if he can even stand to look at you these days. Again, he could pay for this service too.

- Someone to correct when words like "pacific" are used in place of "specific". Or when a letter is written and for example, "computer" is spelled like "cumputer". Someone who is submissive and that he can have power over and instruct like a child – because that's what you are.

- A placeholder human being that he can coddle when you break down in tears every day remembering what a victim you are of your childhood, when you attempted once to be a professional, and of course how normal, every-day life and the people in it were out to get you or hurt you.

I want you to know that you are a disgusting individual. You were an adult and you tried to take advantage of me. I have always been stronger than you and I always will be. You will die weak, non accomplished and with no legacy – This means that upon your exit you will be lost and forgotten to all of time.

You robbed me of my childhood. You continue to rob me of having a relationship with my father. You should be ashamed of that. Instead, I know you are proud of that. It is a shame that that man is too weak to see all of your evil and lies throughout your marriage. My hope is that one day he wakes up.

I won. Although I was forced to call you "mom", you were never my mom. Gavi.

The author reflects...

I am Michael A Delitala and I have labeled myself as "The Revisionist".

In fact, I am little Gavi in this story and every word written in these pages is the truth.

It has to be, otherwise, I must suffer from some variant of the Oedipus complex. My therapist assures me that I absolutely do not suffer from the Oedipus complex.

I wrote this volume to release myself from the burden of the guilt and shame. I wrote this volume in the hopes that if you happen to relate to something like this, then know that the worst is behind you but you have take action to put it behind you. You have to revisit with your child self and work through it with them.

To be critical of myself, I think I could have included another chapter on just how amazing Grandma was and relive some of those very fond memories. I think it could be a later volume. □

I've re-read this volume four times now and offer this reflection.

There will be many more volumes coming.

This volume was authored from a place of rigorous therapy.

It worked. I'm free. Thank you to my two Dr. Cohens.

If you would like to be in touch with me, I can be reached at michaeldelitala@gmail.com